MEDICINAL

CHEF

The
MEDICINAL
CHEF

Eat your way to
a Healthy Gut

Tackle Digestive Complaints
by Changing the Way You Eat, in 50 recipes

DALE PINNOCK

quadrille

CONTENTS

OUT OF ALL OF THE DAY-TO-DAY ISSUES LIKELY TO BE PRESENTED TO A DOCTOR DURING THEIR DAY IN CLINIC, DIGESTIVE WOES ARE PRETTY MUCH UP THERE AT THE TOP.

In fact, an estimated nine million of us have some kind of digestive issue, whether it's permanent or transient. Around the world, the Brits may be seen as a nation ever-so-slightly obsessed with their digestive functions ...

However, in many ways, this ever-increasing plague of digestive maladies is understandable. Our digestive system is the direct interface between the outside modern world and the inner workings of our bodies. As such, it does get exposed to all sorts of weird and wonderful things. Many of which are really quite alien to it. Barrages of processed, refined, sugary, additive-laden food. Weird sodas. Lots of alcohol. All things which, let's be honest here, are a big part of modern life. There aren't really that many of us that make a conscious effort to avoid too many of these things. But they cause all manner of digestive chaos, from simple irritation, through to outright allergic responses and the triggering of inflammation. And that's just the food.

The digestion is a system that is also highly sensitive to bouts of stress. In a week on modern-day Earth, we go through more stress responses than we have ever been used to throughout evolution. Stress can have a huge negative impact on body systems, especially digestion.

So, despite this consistent assault, can the picture be made any better for those suffering with digestive issues? The simple answer is: yes. With the exception of serious inflammatory bowel disease, most of the common digestive complaints can be eradicated or—at the very least—successfully managed by altering the environment. I don't mean living in an Eco dome. I mean changing the internal environment to which the digestive system is exposed. Given the right circumstances, the digestive system is a rapidly self-correcting system. We are beginning to understand a great deal more about causes and triggers of modern-day digestive issues, and simple changes in diet often prove very effective. So that's what this book does. It deals with the more common digestive issues that plague us. It gives you an overview of the dietary strategies to combat them, then brings this information together with tasty, easily adapted recipes.

THE DIGESTIVE SYSTEM

I feel that the best way to understand your health concerns is to find out more about the way in which your body works, and how things can begin to change when problems arise. This is a recurrent theme throughout my work, and justifiably so. This knowledge will help you to develop that kind of understanding of your body that will allow you to make better, more informed choices in the long term and get a better handle of what may be going on inside you. We are going to explore how the digestive system works, so you can get the full picture of what is happening where, and what may be becoming problematic for you. Obviously, if this is all familiar to you, then move on. If not, do take the time to read through this section, as it will really help you make sense of everything. It is only the basics so don't worry, it won't be reams of science, just an overview to help you put all the pieces together.

What is the digestive system? Well, in the simplest of terms, it is there to convert the food we eat into substances that can actually enter our body safely and perform a myriad of functions. When food is first eaten, it cannot enter the body beyond the digestive tract; indeed, if it did, it would trigger an allergic reaction the extent of which you wouldn't believe. The food has to go through a series of transformations in order to extract individual nutrients and nutrient complexes that can leave the digestive tract safely and make their way to cells and tissues where they can be put to use.

THE MOUTH

This is obviously the first stage in the digestive process, as our food makes its way through the digestive system, subject to all manner of processes in order for us to glean nutrients from what we eat. The first element that takes place here is, of course, mechanical digestion: chewing. This breaks the food down into small pieces so there is more surface area exposed for digestive secretions—enzymes and other compounds—to begin working on. This increasing of surface area to maximize digestive capacity is a recurring theme throughout our digestive system. Digestion is quite a taxing activity for the body, so it has to make it as efficient as possible to save energy and be sure it doesn't miss out on important nutrients. Chewing is a vital part of the process, but you'd be amazed at how few people actually chew their food properly. It is definitely worthwhile making an effort to chew food better. Now, don't worry, I'm not going to start sounding like a lot of those other "health" books and tell you to chew every mouthful 30 times. I tried. It is boring, impossible to stay mindful of, and really quite unpleasant, unless of course you want to look like one of Pavlov's dogs and drool uncontrollably! Just a conscious effort not to wolf food down or inhale it is enough.

Mechanical digestion isn't the only thing to take place in the mouth. There is some subtle chemical digestion going on as well. In the mouth, we produce saliva. This is around 90 percent water, but it does contain some mild digestive enzymes, too. The main player here is salivary amylase. This can begin to break down some of the more simple sugars that can be absorbed very quickly. You can experience this first hand when you eat something like a piece of bread or potato. Chew it a few times and you will see it starts to get sweeter. This is salivary amylase in action, liberating the simple sugars that we detect as sweetness. Saliva is also used to lubricate the food to make it easier to swallow. The food-saliva mixture, called the bolus, moves from the mouth down to the esophagus.

THE ESOPHAGUS

The esophagus is a flexible, muscular tube that runs between the mouth and the stomach. It has no role to play in physical digestion or absorption. It is merely a transport system that connects two regions of the digestive tract. This adequate spacing of the stomach and mouth is for a good reason, because stomach secretions are very corrosive and could quickly damage membranes in the mouth —and of course our teeth—so the two are best kept apart. The inner surfaces of the esophagus secrete a thin mucus to aid in the movement of the bolus from the mouth to the stomach.

THE STOMACH

The stomach is a J-shaped baglike organ that lies beneath the diaphragm. Its main function is to carry out specific mechanical and chemical digestion of food. But it also serves as a holding chamber. It can be viewed as an intermediary between the esophagus and the small intestine, which is where most digestion and absorption takes place. As a meal can very easily be eaten much faster than the intestine is able to break it down and digest it, the stomach holds the meal in its chamber and releases it a little at a time into the small intestine at regular intervals. The stomach is a basically acidic environment, with cells lining its internal surface that both measure the acidity and that secrete hydrochloric acid into the stomach. The main food group to really undertake significant chemical digestion here is protein, but we will come to that a little later.

Soon after food enters the stomach from the esophagus, gentle rippling waves start to move through it every 15 to 25 seconds in a controlled and orchestrated manner. These waves are there to move the food around and continually mix it with the digestive secretions released by the stomach. This action turns the stomach contents into a thinner gloopy mixture called chyme. As chyme makes its way through the stomach, it comes to an area called the pylorus.

Here, there is a ring of muscle called the pyloric sphincter which is almost completely closed and controls the exit of food from the stomach into the small intestine. As the chyme reaches the pylorus, the waves of contraction get more forceful and force a few ounces (milliliters) of chyme at a time out from the stomach and into the intestine. This drip-feeding of chyme into the intestine makes digestion more manageable and effective, as the intestine can only effectively deal with a small amount of food at a time.

THE PANCREAS

The pancreas is a gland around 4½ to 6 in (12 to 15 cm) long that lies just behind the stomach. It produces a whopping 1¼ to 1½ quarts (1.2 to 1.5 liters) of pancreatic juices every single day; quite an impressive feat for such a small organ. This juice is a clear, colorless liquid that consists mostly of water, some salts, sodium bicarbonate, and an array of enzymes. The sodium bicarbonate content makes it alkaline. Remember that the stomach is an acidic environment, so anything leaving it is going to be very acidic, too, which can potentially damage other areas of the digestive tract. When pancreatic juice mixes with chyme that has just left the stomach via the pyloric sphincter, it neutralizes the acidic juices in the chyme. The small intestine is an alkaline environment and this initial mixing prepares it for that environment. The enzymes in pancreatic juices include a carbohydrate-digesting enzyme called pancreatic amylase, protein-digesting enzymes including trypsin and chymotrypsin, and the main fat-digesting enzyme called pancreatic lipase, to name but a few.

Pancreatic juice enters the small intestine at the top via the pancreatic duct, which joins with the common bile duct. These two substances flow into the intestine at the same time and in the same location as chyme, as chyme exits the stomach. Bile also increases the alkalinity of chyme.

THE DIGESTIVE SYSTEM

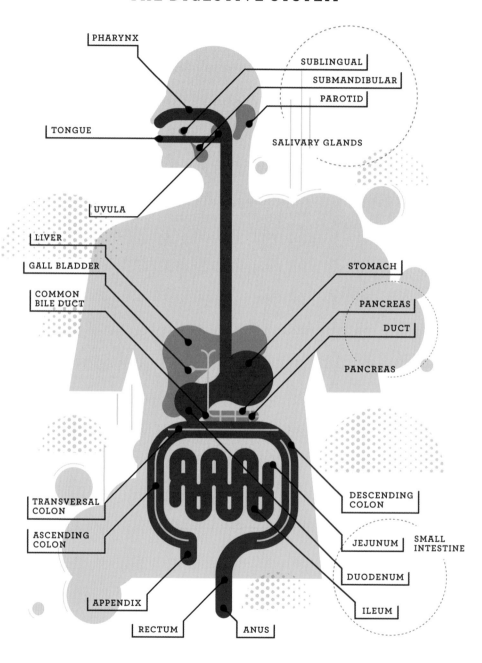

PHARYNX

SUBLINGUAL

SUBMANDIBULAR

PAROTID

SALIVARY GLANDS

TONGUE

UVULA

LIVER

GALL BLADDER

STOMACH

COMMON
BILE DUCT

PANCREAS

DUCT

PANCREAS

TRANSVERSAL
COLON

DESCENDING
COLON

ASCENDING
COLON

JEJUNUM

SMALL
INTESTINE

DUODENUM

APPENDIX

ILEUM

RECTUM

ANUS

THE LIVER AND GALL BLADDER

The liver is the heaviest gland in the body, weighing in at about
3¼ lb (1.5 kg). The gall bladder is a pear-shape sac that sits in a
depression at the rear of the liver. The functions of the liver are
incredibly vast and go way beyond the scope of simple digestive
function. It manufactures proteins; breaks down, metabolizes, and
removes toxins, and pools nutrients. Second to the brain, the liver is
the most important organ in the body. To be honest, the liver's roles
are so vital for survival, that I'd say the liver is of equal importance.
In terms of digestive function, the liver is the manufacturing site for
bile. The hepatocytes (liver cells) can secrete 1¾ to 2 pints (800 ml
to 1 liter) of bile every single day. This fluid is composed of bile
acids, bile salts, cholesterol, a substance called lecithin, and other
metabolic products. The odd thing about bile is that it is half
digestive juice, half excretory substance (it carries waste products
out of the liver to the bowel for removal). The salts found in bile help
to emulsify fats. This means that it breaks them down into small
droplets, which pancreatic lipase then sets to work on. When fats
are in smaller droplets like this, it is easier for the body to break
them down and digest them, rather than chipping away at one big
oil slick. Bile is released into the upper part of the small intestine
when chyme enters it after leaving the stomach. The acidity
of the chyme stimulates the secretion of a hormone called
cholecystokinin, which causes a contraction of the wall of the
gall bladder, which in turn squeezes bile out through the duct.

THE SMALL INTESTINE

The longest part of the digestive tract, this is a mass of coiled,
curled, convoluted folds of tubing. It is made up of three regions: the
duodenum, the jejunum, and the ileum. It is the part of the digestive
tract where most digestion and absorption take place, so the inner
surfaces of the small intestine are designed to maximize this effort.
The inner surface is made up of millions of fingerlike projections.

"The moment you put something in your mouth, there is an impact on your health, positive or negative. When something goes wrong with the digestive system, the whole body can be affected."

DR. MOSARAF ALI

This increases the amount of surface area of the intestine that is available for absorption of nutrients. Inside these fingerlike projections are blood vessels that can carry off nutrients, and specialized lymphatic vessels called lacteals that absorb and transport fats. On the surface of each of these fingerlike projections are millions of microscopic fingerlike projections called microvilli. These extend surface area further, enhancing the extent to which nutrients can be absorbed during their movement through the intestine. As the food moves through the intestine, there are a series of regimented, rhythmical contractions and movements in the intestinal wall. These movements mix chyme with digestive juices and ensure that food particles and nutrients come into contact with the absorbent surfaces of the intestine as much as possible.

There are many different enzymes within intestinal secretions that break down different food groups, such as amylase, sucrase, and lactase for sugar and carbohydrate digestion, trypsin and chymotrypsin for protein digestion, and lipase for fat digestion. I will give a bit more detail later about how different food groups are digested. Once these nutrients are liberated from the food that we have eaten, they are absorbed in different ways. Simple sugars and fats move through the gut wall by means of simple diffusion, meaning they easily just pass through. Simple sugars go into the bloodstream via tiny veins in the villi, while fats diffuse through into specific lymphatic vessels called lacteals. Amino acids, the building blocks for proteins, get absorbed by "active transport." This means that specialized carrier structures on the surface of the villi bind to them and carry them through, again taking them to the liver.

THE LARGE INTESTINE

The large intestine really has a lot less to do with digestion and breakdown in comparison to the other regions of the digestive tract; it is more a site for last-minute absorption and taking what is left behind and moving it on out! When chyme leaves the small intestine and moves to the large, one of the first things that happens is that the remaining water in the chyme begins to get absorbed through the intestinal wall. About 90 percent of the water will be absorbed in the small intestine, but a great deal of what remains will get absorbed via the large intestine. This makes the chyme more solid and it becomes ... you guessed it ... feces. The walls of the large intestine are really geared up for moving things along ready for removal from the body. They are much smoother than those of the small intestine. The most prominent features in the wall of the large intestine are mucus-secreting glands that lubricate its contents, to ease their passage through. The other notable feature is the muscularity of its walls. These muscles contract forcefully, in rhythmical waves called peristalsis (which occurs throughout the whole digestive tract, but more forcefully in the large intestine) which move things along.

The most important aspects of digestion that occur in the large intestine are carried out by things that I personally view as being another digestive organ. These additional unsung heroes of the digestive tract are the gut flora.

"Gut flora" refers to the diverse bacterial population that thrives within our digestive system. The digestive tract is not a sterile tube; it is in fact home to a vast network of bacterial life. This may sound a bit horrific, but we actually have an absolutely vital and symbiotic (mutually beneficial/dependent) relationship with this complex bacterial colony. Believe it or not, there can be 300 to 1,000 different species of bacteria living in the gut. These bugs help us in so many ways. One of the simplest tasks they do is break down certain types of carbohydrate that would otherwise be unusable for the body.

They do this by a process called saccarolytic fermentation, which turns carbohydrates into short chain fatty acids that then go on to help cellular metabolism, nutrient absorption, and even localized tissue repair. Encouraging this process is actually a specific therapeutic target for certain digestive issues and you will see that discussed later in this book. There is some evidence to suggest that bacterial production of short chain fatty acids can prevent inflammatory bowel disease, while certain types of bacteria are believed to have a localized anti-inflammatory/inflammatory mediatory function.

The "good bacteria," as they have become known, have a further defensive role to play. For a long time they were known to be a vital part of immunity within the gut, as they were one of the first barriers between pathogens entering via the digestive tract and the inner workings of the body. They offer an immediate and localized defense. However, in recent years we have realized that the effect of gut flora on immunity goes far beyond just a local influence. We now know that the bacterial colony of the gut can influence immunity systemically. Literally, bacteria in your gut can influence a white blood cell in your little toe. We also now know that gut flora is involved in immunological development in infants and children. The gut flora, is in my opinion, one of the most vital aspects of overall gut health and, no matter what digestive issue I am working with, supporting gut flora is always part of my protocol.

THE DIGESTION OF NUTRIENTS

It may not be 100 percent necessary to know all the ins and outs about digestion but certainly having a firm grasp of the basics will, as I always try to emphasize, give you a good overview as to what is happening in your body on a daily basis, which always helps you to make just a little more sense of what may be going wrong if you have specific concerns.

CARBOHYDRATES AND THEIR DIGESTION

Carbohydrates are the macronutrients supplied by a lot of our starchy staple foods, such as bread and potatoes. Carbohydrates come in all shapes and sizes and really do consist of the good, the bad, and the ugly. The bottom line, though, is that carbohydrates are digested to release their smallest components: sugars! All the carbohydrates that we consume vary in terms of their structure and complexity. Some carbohydrate-rich foods are made up of a lot of fiber, with very few actual digestible elements that can be absorbed as sugars. Others are very simple, either sugars that are ready or almost-ready for immediate utilization, or foods that require very little digestive effort for your body to liberate their sugars. The more complex carbohydrates are called polysaccharides, meaning they are a very complex bundle of lots of sugars bound together (poly = many, saccharide = sugar). The more simple variety tend to come in the form of disaccharides, while the simplest of all sugars are the monosaccharides such as glucose.

MOUTH:

Carbohydrate digestion starts in the mouth. When we chew a food, we secrete saliva. This serves two specific purposes. First, it softens the food and lubricates it in order to make it easier to swallow. Second, saliva contains a useful enzyme called salivary amylase.

This enzyme kick-starts the first steps of carbohydrate digestion. It begins to break starches down into disaccharides. You may have noticed that, when you chew something such as a baked potato, you detect a sweetness pretty quickly. This sweetness is the sugars being released by salivary amylase. This enzyme by no means liberates all the sugars, it merely takes some of the burden off of enzymes further down the line.

STOMACH:

Very little digestion of carbohydrate takes place in the stomach. The stomach is an acidic environment and there are no enzymes present in stomach juices to break the complex bonds of polysaccharides. The acid can, however, break the disaccharide sucrose (the granulated stuff you'd put in to your tea) into the monosaccharides fructose and glucose. Depending on the composition of a meal, foodstuffs can stay in the stomach for anywhere up to six hours (though the average time is just three to four). Food will leave in dribs and drabs. As soon as the food leaves the stomach, it enters the small intestine, where carbohydrate digestion continues.

SMALL INTESTINE:

Once food leaves the stomach, it enters the small intestine. At this stage the pancreas releases its juice, which contains an enzyme called pancreatic amylase (the rock-hard big brother of salivary amylase), which splits polysaccharides (depending on composition) into disaccharides: sucrose, lactose, and maltose being the most common. As these travel through the small intestine, the intestinal walls start to secrete more specific enzymes called sucrase, lactase, and maltase that split these disaccharides into their monosaccharide components, ready for absorption. Sugars pass through the villi in the gut wall, straight into circulation via the venules (small, specifically shaped veins) within the villi.

This is referred to as "simple passive transport," which means they can just flow through the gut wall on their own and don't require any specific assistance getting where they need to go, unlike some nutrients. They diffuse through, then get into circulation.

LARGE INTESTINE:
Some of the more complex fibrous carbohydrates, that don't get degraded too much by pancreatic enzymes and intestinal secretions, do get broken down to a certain extent in the large intestine. As we have seen, this is the home to a massive array of bacterial life. These bugs play a vast array of important roles, but one of the things that they can do is ferment and break down certain complex carbohydrates. This fermentation causes the release of further sugars, but probably the most important thing that arises is the release of certain types of fatty acids that are created during fermentation. An example of this is a fatty acid called butyric acid. These substances can actually repair areas of damage in the digestive tract and maintain the overall health of digestive tract tissue. So, this process of carbohydrate digestion is more about intestinal housekeeping. I find this truly fascinating.

Once carbohydrates have been broken down into their smallest components, they are either sent into the bloodstream or stored as glycogen (the storage form of glucose) in our liver and muscles. The more dense, indigestible carbohydrates are what we commonly refer to as dietary fiber and these ensure that everything moves along nicely through the digestive tract and keep you regular!

PROTEINS AND FATS
Proteins can be incredibly complex, or relatively simple. Their digestion, however, will always be the same. The body will break them down into their smallest building block components: amino acids. These amino acids will either be used directly in the body, or they will be used in the manufacture of specific human proteins.

Amino acids are held together by strong internal bonds, that need breaking before the substances—true building blocks of life—can be utilized by the body.

Fats are really not the demonic dietary substances that we have been led to believe. They are in fact completely and utterly vital for human health. We just need the right sorts. Fats come into the body in very large globules that need breaking down into smaller particles before they can be absorbed.

STOMACH:

The stomach is perfectly geared up for protein digestion. It is a highly acidic environment. The hydrochloric acid in the stomach combines with something called pepsinogen to form a substance called pepsin, which begins to break the bonds that hold the protein together. Some of the more simple proteins can begin to be broken into their individual amino acids (the building blocks that combine to make proteins) at this stage.

All proteins will take a bit of a battering in the stomach. Even if they aren't completely broken down, this immersion in acidic secretions and proteolytic (protein digesting) enzymes will, as you might expect, get them well on their way. Most, however, have to move on to the small intestine.

Fats, on the other hand, are only marginally affected by stomach secretions. Enzymes called lipases begin to break fats down to a lesser degree but, for the most part, fat digestion takes place in the small intestine.

Both of these dietary components cause the stomach to work quite hard to break them down and so can stay in the stomach for some time. Their presence slows down the movement of food from the stomach to the intestine, especially in comparison to a simple carbohydrate meal, for example.

SMALL INTESTINE:

Once the food has left the stomach (which can really take some time with high-quality proteins and fiber), protein digestion is undertaken by two enzymes: trypsin and chymotrypsin. These enzymes break proteins down into amino acids that require a special type of absorption through the digestive tract wall. Unlike the sugars that are released in carbohydrate digestion, amino acids cannot simply diffuse through the wall. They require special transportation structures to actually carry them through the digestive tract wall and into circulation. A process called "active transport." Some amino acids will go straight to specific tissues, but most will be sent to the liver where they are strung together in sequence to make proteins that are needed for the body.

The main part of fat digestion takes place in the small intestine. When fat first leaves the stomach, it is in very large globules that are way too large to be absorbed, even with the vast surface area found within the small intestine. It has to be broken down into smaller and smaller pieces to make it manageable. Bile that is secreted into the small intestine from the gall bladder breaks large globules of fat into smaller droplets that are easier for the body to deal with. Once these smaller droplets are formed, lipases act on them and break them down into particles that are ready for absorption. These particles are called micelles, which then move through the enterocyte (cells that line the digestive tract) wall. They are then bound to a carrier protein and become what is called a chylomicron. These substances are still large in comparison to other nutrients, too large to enter the local blood vessels. So, instead, they enter specially designed lymphatic vessels called lacteals, where they move through the lymphatic system until they come to blood vessels large enough for them to enter.

THE GUT WALL

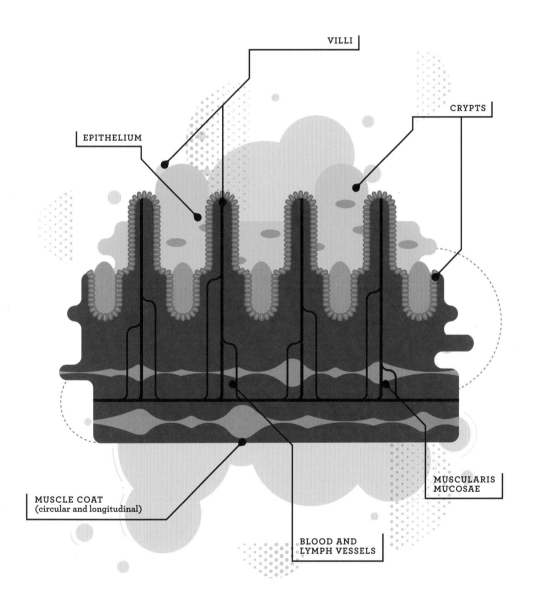

VILLI

CRYPTS

EPITHELIUM

MUSCULARIS
MUCOSAE

MUSCLE COAT
(circular and longitudinal)

BLOOD AND
LYMPH VESSELS

COMMON DIGESTIVE PROBLEMS AND THEIR DIETARY MANAGEMENT

There are, of course, a great number of health problems that may arise in the digestive tract. Not all of them are common and some cannot be managed with diet and require more serious medical intervention. There are a few, though, that are common. I mean really *really* common, affecting millions globally. Thankfully, most of these can be massively responsive to dietary modifications. This book deals with the most common issues that plague the largest amount of people and that are the most responsive to diet.

INTOLERANCE

I'm not going to give this much attention at all. My view on this subject is often not a popular one, but my sole concern is to inform you sensibly and reliably, based on science, not to fall in with the masses. Food intolerances have become a fashionable bandwagon in the nutrition world. Now don't get me wrong, I am not saying that they don't exist, because they certainly do. The problem is they are nowhere near as common as some voices in the health world may have us believe. The world and his wife suddenly think they have one. A real, genuine, full-on intolerance you *really* know about and, as for a full-on allergy, well, that comes with very serious symptoms indeed. My feeling is that often people are diagnosed with intolerances when their digestion is really taking the brunt of modern life. A short run of eating in a hurry, a bit of stress, some disturbed sleep, not enough water, and one vino too many will make you feel like World War III is going on in your digestive tract.

Another thing that makes me insanely angry is some of the ludicrous methods by which people are diagnosed with an "intolerance." The worst of these is a strange contraption that is hooked up to a laptop. You hold a metal "sensor" in one hand, and another metal penlike gizmo is placed on the fingertips of the other hand. This machine then gives you a list of all manner of foods that you had a "response" to. There is such a lack of solid science in this common practice that if it wasn't such a serious matter (of people being conned), it would be laughable.

The only way to figure out if you have an intolerance is to take two steps. The first is give yourself a digestive tune-up (see General tips for great digestion, page 61), then undertake an exclusion diet. This means avoiding the suspected foodstuff for at least six weeks. Then reintroduce it and see what happens. If your insides resemble nuclear fallout, then yes, that food is not for you. If not, it is safe to say the food wasn't the problem and that taking steps to improve your digestive heath has eased your discomfort.

BLOATING (PRIMARY)

Bloating is one of the biggest digestive complaints presented to doctors, dietitians, and nutritional practitioners. When I say primary bloating, I am referring to bloating that is not a symptom of any other condition such as inflammatory bowel disease. Your first port of call is to work with your doctor to ensure that there are no other reasons for your discomfort. However, in most cases, I'd say it is more likely that your diet and lifestyle have become a little out of kilter. Bloating is something that I should imagine every one of us has experienced to one extent or another: the feeling that the abdomen is very tight and feels notably full. It can look as bad as it feels, too. I have seen clients that literally looked pregnant due to bloating ... and that's not the best look on a guy in their 30s! This discomfort is caused mostly by gas. Temporary bloating can occur after a weekend of indulgence, such as over Christmas. When this bloating is occurring regularly and you have adequately ruled out anything more serious, then it's a sure-fire warning sign that things are not right and your digestion needs a tune-up.

Potential causes of primary bloating:

POOR GUT MOTILITY AND CONSTIPATION

In my experience, poor gut motility and/or constipation is one of the leading causes of primary bloating. Gut motility refers to the healthy movement of gut contents along their journey. This continual movement is caused by the rhythmic contraction of muscle in the digestive tract wall. If this motility suffers, the natural movement of gut contents will slow down and things can become a little bunged up, so to speak. This is just one cause of constipation. Poor diet, stress, and dehydration can all cause things to grind to a halt and leave us out of sorts. When this happens, you start to feel bad pretty quickly. You feel heavy, full, headachy, fatigued, and moods can take a nosedive! The biggest discomfort, though, is bloating. As waste builds up in the lower intestine, the bacterial population of the digestive tract will begin to work away on it, causing fermentation of many of the substances in the gut contents, which will in turn cause the release of gas. This gas can become trapped, as its usual exit route starts to get blocked off. This situation can build and begin to get very uncomfortable indeed.

LOW STOMACH ACID

As we have seen, the stomach is a very acidic environment. This is what is needed to break complex proteins down into simpler structures that pancreatic enzymes can easily deal with. If, for whatever reason, stomach acid gets too low, then proteins do not get broken down to the extent they should. This means that, when food leaves the stomach and enters the small intestine, there will be proteins that will be less digested than normal, so pancreatic enzymes may not be able to finish the job adequately. What is the consequence of this? Well, it means partially digested proteins can enter the large intestine, where bacteria will attempt fermentation processes, but cause putrefaction of the proteins. These proteins may also cause localized irritation, too. The result is an aggressive fermentation-type reaction, which creates gas and discomfort.

LOW DIGESTIVE ENZYMES

As we found earlier, when food leaves the stomach and enters the small intestine, an array of enzymes set to work to break it down into the smallest possible denominations ready for absorption. Some circumstances can affect these enzymes. Their production may be down-regulated, or their secretion may be affected by, for example, inflammation in the small intestine (which may be chronic or acute). This can affect the ability of a tissue to secrete an enzyme, or inhibit their release. This again can cause incomplete digestion of certain food groups, causing a chaotic response to them by gut flora when they arrive at the large intestine ... causing gas.

POOR GUT FLORA

One factor that is certainly an issue for those of us living on the Western diet of refined carbohydrates, sugar, and convenience foods is a gut flora that is in a very poor state indeed.

The bacterial colony of the digestive tract, as previously outlined, regulate so many aspects of digestive health and are there to break down some of the foodstuffs we eat that cannot be broken down by enzymes. They also regulate aspects of gut motility, not to mention take care of the digestive tract tissue.

When gut flora suffers, other opportunistic organisms can begin to flourish in the digestive tract. These can cause all manner of problems, from quite ferocious fermentation reactions (meaning gas), through to immunological issues.

Nutritional action plan for bloating:

DRINK MORE WATER

OK, I know this may sound like a weak recommendation or a cop out but, believe me, this is one of the best first steps that you can take. It is all about digestive tract transit! We all know we should eat more dietary fiber to help keep ourselves regular (I will discuss the reasons for this next).

Well, this fiber is useless if we are dehydrated. This is because water is needed to make it swell up and do its job. Now, there are all sorts of weird and wonderful recommendations as to how much water we should drink. Some say eight to 10 glasses, some say as much as three quarts/three liters (wow).

The truth is, we are all different, so our needs always vary. But you can use your body as a great barometer. Simply keep drinking until your urine runs clear. At this point, stop. Once the color begins to return to the urine, drink a little more until the color goes again. Following this guide will keep you hydrated.

INCREASE DIETARY FIBER

Dietary fiber is one of the real keys to keeping everything moving in the digestive tract. The movement of gut contents through the digestive system is governed by a series of rhythmical contractions of the gut wall, called peristalsis, that squeeze the gut wall and slide everything along. Many things affect peristalsis, such as enzymes and hormones, but one of the chief regulators is the digestive tract actually being aware that it has sufficient content within it to give a contraction. This message is relayed by stretch receptors. These receptors measure the stretch of the digestive tract wall, as its contents move through it. When these receptors are stimulated, the digestive tract responds by giving a peristaltic contraction.

I have mentioned the importance of water. Well, water and fiber come together here. Water causes dietary fiber to swell, as fiber can take up a lot of it. The more it swells, the greater the stimulation of the stretch receptors, the greater the stimulation of peristalsis. High-fiber foods aren't necessarily the dull-as-dishwater bran cereals of 1990s fame. They are basically whole foods. Foods in their real state. Fruits, vegetables, low-glycemic grains, and legumes. The more of these you get in the better. It is worth mentioning here that there may be some individuals that are sensitive to a group of compounds found in some high-fiber foods, called FODMAPs (see page 43). These can cause aggressive gas and bloating in some susceptible people, but luckily are easy enough to avoid.

NURTURE YOUR GUT FLORA

I stand by the statement that every lower digestive issue will benefit drastically by improving the bacterial colony in the digestive tract. They regulate and maintain so much, I can't think of a single situation where this wouldn't be relevant. In bloating, getting gut flora in good shape can work wonders, believe me! There are two ways of doing this and I advise both. The first is obviously to add more. I personally wouldn't bother with those little yogurt drinks.

Aside from being sugar bombs, the paltry levels of the bacteria that they actually contain most likely offer very little clinical benefit. I recommend getting a good-quality supplement from your local health food store (see page 47), a type that is a mixed culture (so has more than one type of bug in it) and take it twice a day. One with a meal, and one on an empty stomach. (The reason for this is that there is compelling evidence for both ways of taking it. So much so that I can't actually make up my mind which would be the most suitable, so I recommend both to hedge my bets!) The next step is to feed the bacterial colony that is already there and encourage its growth and flourishing. This is done by consuming foods that are prebiotic. This means they contain specific types of polysaccharide that, when the bacteria ferment them, causes the bacterial colony to reproduce and grow and also to synthesize compounds such as butyric acid that can help to repair the walls of the digestive tract.

USE CARMINATIVES FOR SYMPTOMATIC RELIEF

The word carminative is old herbal terminology. In the most part, my approach is pharmacological and food based, but there are times when I revisit my herbal medicine heritage. Carminatives are basically herbs (or indeed foods, as many turn out to be) that soothe the digestive tract, ease griping, reduce the production of gas, and disperse gas. These ingredients all generally have a very high concentration of specific volatile oils, responsible for their distinctive aromas and flavors, that are responsible for these actions. So powerful are these ingredients that one of them, peppermint, is regularly recommended for chronic bloating and gas by physicians.

TOP INGREDIENTS TO EASE BLOATING

Apples
Packed with fiber, including a very strong soluble fiber called pectin. This is something that makers of jam may be familiar with, as it is used as a thickening agent. The pectin forms a gel-like substance in the digestive tract and takes on more water. This swells up and helps everything move on through.

Artichokes
High in fiber, which aids the movement of gut contents through the digestive tract. Artichokes also contain a compound called caffeoylquinic acid, which stimulates both the production and the release of bile from the liver. Bile is the body's own natural laxative, offering lubrication of the contents of the digestive tract and thus causing easy movement through the tract.

Bananas
Again, these are very high in fiber, helping to move things on nicely by taking on water and swelling up in the digestive tract, stimulating stretch receptors which then stimulate peristalsis. Bananas do have a reputation for becoming a bit laxative so don't go bananas!

Beans
You don't need me to tell you that these are very high in dietary fiber, in fact they are probably some of the highest fiber foods out there. Some of their fibers are composed of quite rugged and persistent polysaccharides. These are the variety that get fermented by the bacteria that live within the digestive tract. This gives beans a double whammy effect. Firstly, their high fiber content will physically give bulk to the gut contents, stimulating the peristaltic movement that will shift them along and out. Secondly, the fermentable polysaccharide content of beans will, over time, enhance the bacterial colony within the digestive tract, which can work absolute wonders for bloating over the long term.

However, for patients whose bloating is associated with IBS (discussed later), beans are not suitable for the FODMAP-sensitive (see page 43).

Cardamom

This is an effective carminative (see page 30). It will help to relax the gut wall and can also rapidly ease the discomfort and full feeling of bloating. This action is delivered by the strong volatile oils that are present in cardamom, the same oils that also give its distinctive flavor.

Caraway seeds

Another effective carminative. These have often formed a major part of traditional herbal teas for infant griping. As with all carminatives, their action is thanks to their unique flavor, or rather the oils responsible for this specific taste.

Jerusalem artichokes

These vegetables have a bit of an identity crisis. They are, in fact, not artichokes at all and —oddly enough—have absolutely nothing whatsoever to do with Jerusalem! They do, however, have something of a reputation for having an ... *interesting* effect upon the digestive system and, the first time that you eat them, you may think that I have played the mother of all practical jokes on you. But fear not, I haven't. I recommend them for good reason. They contain a one of the most powerful prebiotic polysaccharides in the vegetable kingdom. So much so that, the first time you eat them, it may feel like warfare has erupted in your innards. But if you are brave enough, stick with it. This dramatic series of digestive events is the polysaccharide being fed upon by the gut flora. This will be like giving these bugs Champagne and Viagra: reproductive mayhem will ensue. The numbers of bacteria in the digestive tract will increase massively. While the initial onslaught may be full-on, the effect it will have on long-term digestive health is wonderful. Remember, the better the bacterial colony function, the better your symptoms will be long term.

Mint

Probably the most effective and widely documented carminative of them all. Mint has been used in countless clinical trials, in both its crude whole plant form and as a high-strength extract. The oils that give you that cooling sensation in your mouth interact with receptors in the digestive tract wall that cause muscular relaxation. This can ease and soothe the digestive tract and have an almost instant effect upon bloating. Try a cup or two of peppermint tea during a flareup and see what I mean.

Onions

Another ingredient that is part of the long-term management of bloating. This is because onions are an effective prebiotic. This is thanks to a compound they contain called inulin, which basically works like a food source for the good bacteria in the gut. As they feed on it, they begin to replicate and the colony gets stronger. If you are an IBS sufferer though, onions are unsuitable for the FODMAP-sensitive (see page 43).

Sweet potatoes

One of my favorite staple ingredients. Sweet potatoes are very high in fiber, helping to move things through the digestive tract so that they don't hang around long enough for too much fermentation to occur. Sweet potatoes also contain prebiotic polysaccharides that will support growth of gut flora.

CONSTIPATION

Constipation is a big issue. It basically means that you are going to the toilet less frequently or that, when you do go, it is difficult and sometimes painful. Everyone is different, but in general it is usual to open your bowels one to three times a day. There is an old saying that it should be after each meal. I have seen people in clinic that can go a week to 10 days between bowel movements. This is constipation at its worst and the side effects are dreadful. The occasional bout of it is totally normal and everyone gets bunged up from time to time. The real problem is when it becomes a chronic issue.

Potential causes of constipation:

NOT ENOUGH FIBER

As discussed, fiber is vital for keeping everything moving through the digestive system. It gives the gut contents their bulk and swells up to stimulate stretch receptors, which in turn stimulate peristaltic waves that move everything along. So many of us are not getting anywhere near the amount of fiber that we should; in fact, some people can go for days and days without consuming any.

NOT DRINKING ENOUGH

Fiber is only one part of the picture when it comes to keeping the gut moving properly. A high fiber intake is only as good as the amount of fluid you drink. Fiber delivers its beneficial actions by absorbing water and swelling up as a result, sometimes to many times its original size. It is this swelling that stimulates the stretch receptors, which then go on to stimulate peristalsis.

LACK OF EXERCISE

Believe it or not, our activity levels can have a huge impact here. The evidence is unclear as to how exactly this influences gut motility, but it appears likely that physical activity may have some kind of influence on peristalsis, or physical movement of the gut contents. There may also be a stress-reducing link here. Studies have certainly shown that patterns of higher activity do indeed decrease digestive transit time and reduce constipation. Another reason to get out there and get moving. You don't have to become a marathon runner, just go for a brisk walk. Take a dance class. Do whatever you feel comfortable doing. Just do something!

OTHER FACTORS THAT AFFECT GUT MOTILITY

There are other things that have been recorded as factors that can affect gut motility, although the reasons why aren't always as clear:

Excessive calcium supplementation

Some painkillers

Iron supplements in the ferrous sulfate form

Stress

Nutritional action plan for constipation

EAT MORE FIBER—SOLUBLE AND INSOLUBLE
Fiber is definitely the key but, before you go munching down pounds of bran, there are two types, and increasing both can make things much more comfortable. These are soluble and insoluble fibers. Soluble fiber will actually form a soft gel-like texture in the digestive tract. This really helps to soften everything. If the stool has become very compact and hard, you are really going to want to soften things up and make life easy for yourself. Insoluble fiber lives up to its name. It is fiber that doesn't really break down much at all. It will absorb water, but remains pretty much unchanged. This is what used to be referred to as roughage.

INCREASE WATER INTAKE
This one is straightforward enough. As I have mentioned before, rather than just aiming for some random number of units of water to drink, just drink until your urine runs clear, then stop. When color returns to it, drink a little more ... and on it goes.

TOP INGREDIENTS TO EASE CONSTIPATION

Apples

These are just fantastic for digestive health, especially for those people suffering from constipation. This is because they contain a unique soluble fiber called pectin. This fiber forms a gel-like substance that swells up in the digestive tract, takes on lots of water, and softens the stool, making it easier to pass.

Beans

These contain both soluble and insoluble fiber.

Chia seeds

These have become something of a fashionable ingredient of late, and all manner of weird and wonderful desserts and treats containing them are popping up in grocery and health food stores. There are some really weird and daft claims made about them, but what is indisputable is that they are a great ingredient for gut health, especially if you want to maintain healthy gut motility. They are packed with a gel-like soluble fiber that swells to many times its size. I don't know if you have ever tried adding chia seeds to a drink or put them on cereal or anything like that, but if you have you will notice that in a matter of minutes they develop this strange jellylike texture. Well, that is the gel in the coating of the seeds taking on water at lightning speed. This gives you an idea as to how they are going to act in the digestive tract. If you take these and drink enough water, it can be like having your very own in-house chimney sweep!

Dates

A great sweet treat for those moments when you want to reach for a sugary snack, as they pack a lot of nutrients along with their sweetness. They are also very high in fiber. But watch out, over consumption does have quite the reputation for having dramatic consequences, if you catch my drift!

Eggplant

These are a greatly underrated and often underused vegetable, but one of my favorites, and not just for their satisfying flavor. They are a great source of both soluble and insoluble fibers, which are excellent for constipation sufferers. Again, these fibers will swell in the digestive tract and stimulate the stretch receptors, which will then go on to stimulate peristalsis, the rhythmical waves of muscular contractions in the digestive tract walls that cause its contents to move through with ease.

Oats

Another ingredient that is fantastic for the health of your digestive system and should be included at breakfast time, if possible. They, too, are packed with soluble fiber, this time in the form of something called

beta glucan. Like pectin, beta glucan will form a gel-like substance in the digestive tract that will soften gut contents and comfortably move everything along on its way.

Onions

Just a wonderful ingredient that offers benefits to many different body systems, from the immune to the cardiovascular. Vitally, they contain a prebiotic polysaccharide called inulin. Prebiotic basically refers to something that supports and enhances the growth and development of the bacterial colony within the digestive tract. Anything that improves this colony will have a profound impact upon gut function. This flora will regulate everything from digestive tract contractions to localized repair of digestive tract tissue. Look after it well!

"Gut flora has long been noted for the role it plays in prevention of and defense against diseases. They inhibit the growth of other harmful organisms, and prevent the attachment of pathogens in the digestive tract."

DR. MICHAEL MURRAY

IRRITABLE BOWEL SYNDROME (IBS)

Irritable Bowel Syndrome, or IBS, is becoming incredibly common, or at least its diagnosis is! It was certainly one of the most usual digestive complaints that patients at my clinics presented with, although down the line some were reassessed and ended up with a different diagnosis. It is believed that the condition can affect one in five people. I am not sure how accurate this picture truly is, because IBS is a bit of a tricky customer. It is notoriously difficult to come to a definitive conclusion that a patient is indeed suffering from IBS. This is because there are so many digestive issues that can surface and, in the absence of any test that will give a specific clinical marker for a known condition, the diagnosis is often given. Many digestive problems can deliver the same symptoms, so getting to the bottom of the issue and determining true IBS is fraught with obstacles. True IBS, though, usually presents as bouts of constipation, diarrhea, and accompanying bloating, cramping, and pain. There is no set pattern to this and sufferers can have any combination of symptoms for any period of time. Pain can arise in many different areas of the abdomen and some sufferers report that it is relieved by using the bathroom. The symptoms can be sporadic, with weeks or even months between episodes, while in others the symptoms are as good as constant.

POSSIBLE CAUSES OF IBS

The other thing that makes IBS such a tricky customer is that nobody can be sure what causes it. There are many theories and certainly many strong links, yet none of them are conclusive enough to definitively say "yes, this is the cause." Plus there is a strong argument that IBS may indeed just be an outcome, a response in the digestive tract to certain stimuli or changes, meaning that there may be many possible factors that would instigate a chain of events that would lead to the syndrome.

OVERACTIVITY OF NERVES OR MUSCLES OF THE GUT

Our digestive tract is a very muscular system. The walls of most of the digestive system have varying degrees of muscularity. These muscles are involved in churning, mixing, and moving things along. Like any muscle, they have a supply of nerves to stimulate their contraction. This is all perfectly orchestrated and involves a mixture of signals from the brain and localized hormonal signals to regulate it. It is believed that in some IBS cases, this system can become overactive. It isn't clear whether this overactivity is muscular or neurological, but many people do equate stress with the onset or exacerbation of symptoms. This overactivity can lead to muscular contractions becoming more frequent, leading to rapid expulsion of gut contents and diarrhea. They may become more forceful and cause painful cramping, or they may respond to overstimulation with bouts of reduced contractility (the contracting response), leading to episodes of constipation.

INFECTION

It is estimated that one in six cases of IBS actually arise following an episode of gastroenteritis or infection within the digestive tract. The inflammation and immunological activity that occurs during such infections may potentially trigger the type of sensitivity described above.

FOOD INTOLERANCES

OK, so you have probably gathered that I am not a fan of the food intolerance thing (see page 25). But, in IBS, I actually am far more open to the possibility, as there is a very strong evidence base for a very specific type of food sensitivity. This is to a group of compounds called FODMAPs ...

THE FODMAPS DIET

The FODMAPs diet began in Australia and is now a very hot topic in the nutrition world for the management of IBS. It is used frequently in UK outpatient clinics. Recent research at King's College, London found that it is successful at relieving symptoms in 70 percent of cases. You are probably wondering what on earth a FODMAP is. Well, it is actually an acronym. It stands for: Fermentable Oligosaccharides Disaccharides Monosaccharides, And Polyols! These are certain types of sugars that are very poorly absorbed in the small intestine. They are not simple sugars such as glucose. They are more complex in structure, or of a shape that makes them resilient to digestive enzymes, meaning they move through most of the digestive tract more or less intact. They are poorly absorbed by everyone, but those with IBS seem to have an exaggerated sensitivity. These sugars can sometimes draw water into the bowel which can cause rapid-onset diarrhea. When these sugars get to the large intestine, the local bacterial population begin to ferment them, which causes gas and bloating and sometimes abdominal pain. So, this diet is essentially an exercise in avoiding these problematic substances. They are, however, very widely spread throughout a lot of the foods that we would see as "healthy" ingredients. This can make the diet seem a little restricted and dull. I have developed recipes in this book around the FODMAP diet which aim to show you how, with just a little bit of imagination, you can bring the diet to life.

As these compounds are so widely distributed in foods, it is helpful for most people to see a list of the dos and don'ts that can be used as a daily reference. This will help you to put together your own meal plans and to find ways to improve the foods you are already eating. This table (see overleaf) should be a great starting point. It may seem a little restrictive at first but, with a little bit of experimentation (and my recipes later in the book), you will soon find it second nature to cook the FODMAP way.

EAT

Meat and fish
All

Dairy/fats
Butter
Eggs
Hard cheeses
   (such as Parmesan)
Lactose-free ice creams
   or desserts
Milk substitutes, such
   as nut or rice milks
   or lactose-free milk
Nuts and nut butters
   (but avoid pistachios)
Vegetable oils
Yogurts (if plain and
   low-lactose; see if
   you can tolerate it)

Grains/cereals
Amaranth
Buckwheat
Corn/cornmeal
Millet
Oats
Quinoa
Rice
Tapioca/cassava
Teff

AVOID

Dairy/fats
Creams
Cream cheeses
Ice creams
Milks
Milk products (creamer,
   instant cocoa, and so on)
Soft cheeses
Sweetened or flavored
   yogurts

Grains/cereals
Barley (pearl and pot)
Bulgur wheat
Couscous (contains wheat)
Rye
Semolina (contains wheat)
Wheat and wheat products
   (bread, pasta, cake,
   and so on)

EAT

Vegetables
Baby corn (well-cooked)
Carrots
Celery
Eggplants (though watch out,
   some can't tolerate it)
Green beans
Lettuces
Pak choi/choi sum
Parsnips
Peppers
Potatoes
Rutabagas
Scallions
   (green part only)
Spinach
Squashes
Sweet potatoes/yams
Tomatoes
Zucchini

Fruit
Bananas
Blueberries
Canteloupe melons
Cranberries
Grapefruits
Grapes
Honeydew melons
Kiwis
Lemons/limes
Oranges
Pineapples
Raspberries
Rhubarb
Strawberries

AVOID

Vegetables
Artichokes
Asparagus
Avocados
Beans and legumes
Beets
Broccoli
Cabbages
Cauliflowers
Fennel
Garlic
Mushrooms
Onions
Peas
Shallots
Sugar snaps/snow peas

Fruit
Apples
Apricots
Blackberries
Cherries
Dried fruits (in large
   quantities)
Mangoes
Nectarines
Peaches
Pears
Plums
Prunes
Watermelons

NUTRITION ACTION PLAN FOR IBS

TRY FOLLOWING THE FODMAPS DIET

As discussed (see page 43), this diet as a general eating pattern can
be effective for around 70 percent of sufferers of IBS. The recipes for
IBS sufferers in this book are all FODMAP-friendly, so should give
you a good head start. Using the guide on the previous pages, you
can also start to piece together your own recipes, or tweak
your favorite dishes so they fall in line with FODMAP.

USE A MAGNESIUM SUPPLEMENT

Having magnesium on hand can be very useful during a flareup
of IBS. If you suffer from spasms and abdominal pain, a sudden
burst of magnesium may offer some benefit. It is thought that there
can be an overstimulation of the muscular walls of the digestive tract
in some cases of IBS, causing spasm and pain. Whether it is the
muscles themselves, or the nerves that supply them, this muscular
contraction can at times get out of hand and you really know
about it during an attack. Magnesium works alongside calcium to
regulate muscular contraction. Calcium causes muscles to contract,
whereas magnesium causes muscles to relax. An additional burst
of magnesium can encourage relaxation of that spasm, which is
caused by muscular contraction. This by no means stops the
problem from arising, but can be a very effective part of your
IBS management at home.

NURTURE YOUR GUT FLORA

Usually I recommend a two-fold approach to improving gut flora:
introducing fresh cultures to the body, then encouraging growth and
reproduction of the colony by providing specific types of prebiotic
agents. However, in cases of IBS, where FODMAP sensitivity is
likely, the use of prebiotics is definitely not recommended;
these are the very compounds that are problematic.

So, for IBS, just getting more of the right bacteria in is the key. I recommend getting a broad-spectrum probiotic supplement. This means one that contains many different strains of bacteria. That is important, because different strains regulate different aspects of digestive tract health. *Bifidobacterium,* for example, can regulate peristalsis, the muscular contraction of the digestive tract wall that sometimes goes awry in IBS. Some others can also ease bloating and gas and improve the ability of the digestive tract to deal with some complex polysaccharides. Take the probiotic twice a day, once with a meal and once on an empty stomach. These bacteria can offer so many regulatory effects upon the digestive system that their use is always warranted. The use of probiotics is especially important if you believe that your symptoms arose following an infection.

INFLAMMATORY BOWEL DISEASE (IBD)

Inflammatory bowel disease is the umbrella term given to a group of disorders that cause inflammation throughout the digestive tract. The two most common disorders that come under the IBD umbrella are ulcerative colitis and Crohn's disease. Symptoms of IBD can be any combination of acute or chronic abdominal pain, diarrhea, unexplained weight loss (this must *always* be referred to a doctor), reduced appetite, fever, and bleeding from the bowels (again this must *always* be referred to a doctor, no exceptions).

The two conditions, ulcerative colitis and Crohn's disease, are the most common inflammatory bowel diseases and they are very similar. The biggest difference really is the part of the digestive tract that they affect.

Ulcerative colitis affects the large intestine, although associated symptoms from mouth ulcers to joint problems may also be experienced. This condition causes an inflammation of the wall of the large intestine which gets severe enough for open sores/ulcers to form. These can bleed and in some severe cases get infected and leach pus. This condition can sometimes get so severe that bowel perforations occur, causing peritonitis and demanding immediate emergency surgery.

Crohn's disease on the other hand can affect any part of the gastrointestinal tract, from mouth to anus. In Crohn's, there can be areas of aggressive inflammation and scar tissue that can lead to narrowing of areas of the intestine, and there have been cases where this has caused obstruction. The inflammatory damage to the digestive tract wall can span the entire thickness of the tissue, way beyond just superficial surface damage. These lesions can also ulcerate. There are other rarer conditions that are part of the IBD spectrum. These are collagenous colitis and lymphocytic colitis. As these are rare conditions I won't deal with them here, but some of the principles below will still be of relevance.

In nutritional terms, it is important to remember that with inflammatory bowel disease, more specifically Crohn's disease, damage to the digestive tract wall will affect the sites that absorb nutrients and patterns of malnutrition are very common in those that are affected badly by the condition.

Potential causes of Inflammatory Bowel Disease

AUTOIMMUNITY

It is believed that inflammatory bowel disease is an autoimmune condition. This describes the phenomena of the body's own immune system turning upon itself.

The immune system can develop defensive responses to specific types of the body's own tissues and begin a campaign of attack, by suddenly forming autoantibodies. These are similar to the antibodies that we make against certain pathogens (such as chickenpox) that mean we know what plan of attack to instigate if we are exposed to it again.

As well as this occurring, the regulatory systems that usually keep such mishaps in check begin to fail. In the case of inflammatory bowel disease, this response is hitting the inner lining of the digestive tract and some of the muscular tissue beneath.

There is no one specific cause for autoimmune responses and potential triggers are often the subject of medical debate. Environmental factors may be relevant. Changes in the local environment may trigger an immunological reaction that causes the production of autoantibodies.

There is some evidence that came to light in March 2014 to suggest that patients with Crohn's disease had lower numbers of beneficial bacteria in the digestive tract as well as higher levels of more potentially harmful flora. It is hypothesized that there may be an immunological response to these more problematic flora, which could be the trigger.

GENETICS

There is certainly a strong genetic element to inflammatory bowel disease. It is believed that there are dozens of different genes that may contribute to the onset of the disorders. As with many issues though, genes on their own are unlikely to be the be-all and end-all. It is the interaction between genes and environment that sets the cascade of disease into motion.

Nutrition action plan for Inflammatory Bowel Disease

BALANCE YOUR FATTY ACIDS

Fatty acids are fat-derived compounds that are massively important in human physiology. It is an area with which, as any of you that are familiar with my work will know, I am completely fascinated and marginally obsessed. This is because they are such small compounds that can deliver life-altering changes and their intake in the modern world has really gone down the shoot.

Fatty acids come from the types of fats we consume in our diet. Our diets have changed massively over the last 50 years and, in this age of fat phobia, the types of fats we are consuming has changed massively. Why is the type of fat we consume relevant to IBD? Well, fatty acids are actually used by the body to produce a group of communication compounds called prostaglandins that, among other things, regulate the inflammatory response.

There are three different classes of prostaglandin: Series 1, Series 2, and Series 3. Series 1 and Series 3 switch inflammation off and down-regulate it, whereas Series 2 switches it on and exacerbates it. Series 3 is the most potent anti-inflammatory prostaglandin.

Different types of dietary fat are metabolized to form different prostaglandins. The building blocks for prostaglandins come from fats called omega fatty acids. There are several, but the most important are omega-3—the one that most people will be aware of—and its lesser known cousin, omega-6.

Even though both are important, it is vital that we get the balance right. To cut a long story short, it is important that we get more omega-3 than omega-6.

Omega-6 fatty acids are metabolized to form the powerfully proinflammatory Series 2 prostaglandins. Omega-3 is metabolized to form the anti-inflammatory Series 1 and Series 3 prostaglandins. If we consume more omega-6 than omega-3, we will essentially force-feed the metabolic pathways that manufacture prostaglandins that switch on and worsen inflammation.

The opposite, thankfully, is also true. If we consume more omega-3 than omega-6, then we force-feed the same metabolic pathways to make more of the anti-inflammatory Series 1 and Series 3 prostaglandins.

This small, simple change can have a massive impact upon any inflammatory condition. So, in practice, reducing your omega-6 means avoiding vegetable oils such as sunflower oil, plain vegetable oil, corn oil, and so on, as these are almost pure omega-6. Avoid processed ready meals, potato chips, and junk food as these have so many of these oils.

The easiest way to increase your intake of omega-3 is turn to the oily fish, such as salmon, mackerel, herrings, and so on. These are not only the richest sources of omega-3, but they also have a high proportion of the most active form, EPA, which is rapidly converted in our bodies to help make the potently anti-inflammatory Series 3 prostaglandin.

Plant sources of omega-3 include flaxseeds and chia seeds and walnuts. Do bear in mind, though, that the effects will be much less pronounced and take a little longer to deliver, as the plant form of omega-3—ALA—requires several steps of conversion before it can become the active prostaglandin. Human beings aren't overly successful at performing this transformation when the source is a plant, rather than a fish. We maybe convert 10 percent of ALA that we take in, if we are lucky!

PROBIOTICS AND PREBIOTICS

No matter what the digestive issue, probiotics are always part of the armory, as they regulate so many aspects of digestive health. However, on some occasions, they can have a very specific targeted function. This is certainly the case with Inflammatory Bowel Disease. It is believed that some bacterial strains may offer a direct localized anti-inflammatory activity.

The main benefit of these bacteria, however, comes from when they feed on certain types of sugars. There are some large, complex sugar molecules that actually act as a food source for the good bacteria. These are known as prebiotics. They occur quite broadly in foods such as onions, legumes, root vegetables, and so on. They can also be supplemented; look out for something labeled FOS (Fructo Oligosaccharides). These prebiotic nutrients are fermented by the gut flora as they feed upon them. This fermentation creates compounds known as short-chain fatty acids. These compounds have been found to repair damaged areas of the digestive tract and reduce inflammation. I advise supplementing with probiotics and then eating a wide variety of food sources of prebiotics.

TOP INGREDIENTS TO EASE INFLAMMATORY BOWEL DISEASE

Butternut squash

I love squash. Their sweet flavor and versatility are wonderful. The vegetables are also rich in something called beta-carotene. This is the thing responsible for their bright orange color. Beta-carotene also happens to have an anti-inflammatory activity. This is because it has some antioxidant function, which helps to buffer some of the free radical activity that arises in the body during the inflammatory response.

Ginger

This rhizome has a very long standing reputation as an anti-inflammatory ingredient and has been the subject of a fair bit of research in Europe and the USA. The oils in ginger that are responsible for its pungent spicy flavor and aroma are, as ever, the keys. These interrupt the conversion of something called arachidonic acid into the compounds that stimulate and aggravate inflammation.

Mackerel

This is definitely one of my top ingredients for overall health. It is especially important for inflammatory conditions, thanks to very high levels of omega-3 fatty acids. These vital fats are the body's metabolic building blocks for an important group of compounds known as prostaglandins, which are basically communication molecules. One of their main jobs is to regulate the inflammatory response. There are three types of prostaglandin compounds, two of which are anti-inflammatory because they switch off and dampen down the inflammatory response. One of them is proinflammatory, as it switches on and exacerbates inflammation. Prostaglandins are made from different fats that we consume in our diet. Omega-3 fatty acids, such as those found in oily fish, are metabolized to form the most aggressively anti-inflammatory prostaglandins, those ones known as Series 3. So, long story short, by eating more omega-3 from oily fish, we are forcing our body to produce more of its own natural built-in anti-inflammatory compounds, a must for the self-management of any inflammatory issue.

Onions

A great all-rounder for digestive health. They are a rich source of inulin, a potent prebiotic that encourages the growth and flourishing of the gut flora. Gut flora play an important role in the repair and maintenance of digestive tract tissue, so supporting their growth is a fundamental part of managing any digestive issue.

Pineapple

This fruit contains the anti-inflammatory enzyme called bromelian. This is a potent enzyme that is found in the tougher core of the pineapple. It has been shown to offer an anti-inflammatory activity. It isn't anywhere near as potent as the long-term effects of omega-3, and its effects are transient. However, I think it is a very useful ingredient for your armory.

Salmon

This oily fish is packed with anti-inflammatory omega-3 fatty acids. As I have outlined previously, these vital fats provide the body with the building blocks that it needs to manufacture its own built-in anti-inflammatories, the prostaglandins. Different fats get metabolized to form different prostaglandins. The omega-3 fatty acids found in oily fish get metabolized to form the type of prostaglandin that turns inflammation right down. Consistent consumption of omega-3 fatty acids has been shown to have a massive effect on inflammatory conditions. We aren't talking radical cures here, but very effective, safe self-management. Just eat more salmon! I would add, though, that more of the good bits are found in the better quality fish. You don't need to spend a fortune, but I would recommend buying one of the packs that lie somewhere in the middle.

Sweet potatoes

These are another lovely anti-inflammatory food. This is due to the compounds that make their flesh that orange color: the carotenoids. These are antioxidant compounds, and as such will deliver in the body a certain amount of localized anti-inflammatory activity. OK, it isn't as potent as taking a prescription anti-inflammatory but it is a perfect example of the type of ingredient you can regularly incorporate into your daily diet to deliver a cumulative benefit to the digestive tract.

Turmeric

This lovely eastern spice has quite the reputation for being an anti-inflammatory. This is due to the presence of a group of compounds within it called curcuminoids. These are the substances responsible for turmeric's aggressive lingering yellow color (and the reason you should wear gloves to prepare it, unless you want to look nicotine-stained for a few weeks). Curcuminoids have been shown to interrupt the production of proinflammatory communication compounds. This can reduce inflammation that is already active. While most trials have been conducted with concentrated extracts of turmeric, there have been numerous small-scale trials focusing on normal levels of whole turmeric; that is, levels that would be normally consumed within the diet. These have also mostly shown positive outcomes that, coupled with the spice's safety, makes it an ideal addition to the diet on a regular basis. So eat more Indian food!

REFLUX

Reflux is a very common condition that is thought to afflict 10 to 20 percent of the population. It is also known by other names, such as heart burn or acid indigestion. In short, it involves the movement of acidic stomach secretions that rise from the stomach up into the esophagus. This causes symptoms of sporadic dull burning that we know so well as heart burn. This can be accompanied by bloating, belching, and even small amounts of acidic secretion appearing in the mouth. Unfortunately, the most popular way of dealing with this issue often exacerbates it in the long run. The secretions of the stomach are acidic. They are supposed to be. That's how we were designed. Reflux does not arise because all of a sudden we start to randomly produce more acid. It is caused by the acid that is meant to exist suddenly getting into an area where it is not supposed to be. However, the common way of dealing with reflux or "heart burn" is to take an antacid. Oh yes, this absolutely will give you relief, there is no question of that. But what happens next may actually make matters worse. As I said, the stomach is meant to be acidic. Like all other systems in the body, it is fully aware of itself and constantly self-monitoring, so that if anything goes wrong it can detect it and rectify the situation as soon as possible. When it comes to stomach acidity, this regulation goes on all the time. In the stomach there are groups of cells that sit side by side throughout its lining. One type of cell secretes acid, whereas the neighboring cell measures acidity. The two cell lines "talk" to each other. If, for whatever reason, the acidity in the stomach goes too high, the cells that are measuring it will talk to the cells that secrete acid and tell them to reduce their output. But, of course, the opposite is true, too. If the level of acid in the stomach goes down, then the acid-secreting cells will be encouraged to secrete more to put it right. Can you guess what's coming? When we take antacids, we are reducing the acidity of the stomach. So what happens ...?

The cells that are measuring acidity become aware of this and tell the acid-secreting cells to make much more to correct things. So using antacids can make matters far worse, and is akin to sweeping dirt under the rug.

Potential causes of reflux

WEAKENED GASTROESOPHAGEAL SPHINCTER

This sphincter is a ring of muscle that sits at the very top of the stomach, at the point where the esophagus and stomach meet. This ring of muscle is basically designed to separate the two environments. The stomach is a highly acidic environment and as such its surfaces are built in such a way so as to not be damaged by its acidic secretions. Other tissues, however, are not. That is the primary function of the gastroesophageal sphincter; to keep acidic secretions out of the esophagus. It, of course, also allows for controlled entry of food bolus into the stomach. Whenever this sphincter weakens, its ability to stay closed is diminished and the acidic stomach contents can rise up into the esophagus, causing pain, irritation, and inflammation.

HIATUS HERNIA

Hiatus hernia is one of the most common reasons for prolonged ongoing reflux. A hiatus hernia is where a part of the upper section of the stomach moves through a hole in the diaphragm. This can either be transient, or permanent. Either way, this movement distorts the shape of the stomach. In doing so, it changes the shape of the sphincter that is there to keep stomach contents from entering the esophagus. When this occurs, what was a perfectly sized and shaped piece of muscle changes shape as the stomach distorts. Its ability to close properly and keep stomach contents inside is greatly inhibited, leading to a leaching of acidic stomach secretions in to the esophagus.

WEAKENING OF THE GASTROESOPHAGEAL SPHINCTER
This ring of muscle, as we are now aware, is designed to open as
the bolus of food slides down the esophagus into the stomach, then
remain closed to ensure that acidic stomach secretions don't enter
the esophagus where they can be highly irritating, even corrosive if
uncontrolled secretion persists. The sphincter can be weakened by
certain lifestyle elements. Smoking is a known weakener of this
muscle. Dietary factors such as excess fats (though I feel this is
highly debatable) and also alcohol are believed to weaken the
sphincter temporarily. Persistent intake leads to chronic weakening.
Another dietary factor that is believed to be a causative factor in
some individuals is coffee; however, if anybody takes my morning
espresso away, they better be a good runner.

OVEREATING
The final and most obvious factor that can cause temporary
reflux is overeating. If the stomach is overfilled, this can cause
a temporary distortion of the sphincter.

NUTRITION ACTION PLAN FOR REFLUX

In terms of causative factors, the evidence for a direct causal relationship between a specific food and the onset of reflux just isn't there. So, with that in mind, I have a single targeted approach for reflux sufferers and this is reducing inflammation. Reflux does cause irritation and inflammation in the esophagus. Easing this situation can certainly be achieved through diet. You will notice that there isn't a recipe category for reflux in the book. That is because there are so many recipes that will achieve the objective of reducing inflammation, throughout the whole book, so it is easier for me to list them here.

EAT A VARIETY OF COLORS

I know we have heard this a million times, but brightly colored fruits and vegetables are really a key factor in an anti-inflammatory diet. Different spectrums of color represent different categories of nutrients and phytochemicals. Many of these, particularly the phytochemicals, have antioxidant and anti-inflammatory activity.

BALANCE FATTY ACIDS

As we have learned, we need to eat more omega-3 and less omega-6. This is done by eliminating vegetable oils such as corn, sunflower (also labeled as vegetable oil), soy oils, and so on. Don't go near margarine ever, *ever* and avoid processed foods, which are often filled to the hilt with omega-6. Rely on olive and coconut oils for cooking, as these both contain virtually no omega-6 so don't upset the omega balance. To increase your omega-3 intake, increase your intake of oily fish first and foremost as these are the richest source of the most active forms of omega-3: EPA and DHA. Other food sources include flaxseeds and chia seeds and walnuts, but bear in mind these contain the less active ALA form of omega-3. The best option is to eat the oily fish. If you are vegetarian, seek out one of the algae-derived EPA products that are starting to appear.

RECIPES TO EASE REFLUX:

These recipes really bring the best anti-inflammatory ingredients together and are found throughout the book.

GENERAL TIPS FOR GREAT DIGESTION

If you aren't necessarily suffering from a specific digestive issue, but want to just give your digestion a tune-up or keep it working at its best, these few tips will help you keep everything ship-shape.

DRINK MORE WATER

OK, OK, it's a health book cliché, but it is an important point to drive home. Water is vital for virtually every single aspect of health and especially that of the digestive system.

Dietary fiber, the thing that swells in our digestive tract, stimulating stretch receptors, then, in turn, stimulating peristaltic contractions, require water. They draw water in, which is what makes them swell.

Dehydrated bodies mean dehydrated digestive contents ... and that soon gets very bunged up and unpleasant. So how much? Well, there are all manner of weird arbitrary numbers flying around. But your body gives you a simple indication. Drink water until your urine begins to run clear. At this point, stop drinking water. Once the urine begins to get color back to it, drink some more. This way you will generally stay hydrated. However, if you are taking supplements such as B vitamins that give you the fluorescent yellow laser pee that mask the natural color, then I'd say the general rule of thumb would be a glass every hour or so throughout the normal working day.

EAT WHOLE FOODS

This is the simplest step you can take toward better health overall. This doesn't mean suddenly following any weird dietary regimes. It just means eating real food. That's it. As the saying goes, if it ran, swam, or grew, then eat it. Sadly so many of us are eating stuff that —well—is anything but food. I mean that. A lot of what many people eat today isn't what we are supposed to be eating as food at all.

In my work I come across so, so many people that can literally go for one or two weeks without eating anything that resembles fresh food. Instead they are consuming an array of odd substances found in bright packaging, nuked in the microwave.

Now don't get me wrong, I'm not suddenly demonizing these foods and getting into finger-wagging mode. My issue is with the amount in which they are consumed. Sadly, they dominate our diets, mostly due to the wrong-headed notion that they are somehow convenient or affordable options. Well, heart disease, diabetes, and cancer are pretty inconvenient, I'd say. And as far as affordability is concerned, this really has more to do with very clever and ethically questionable marketing.

Last year I made a documentary for a news program. We worked with two girls who were living in a London YMCA, and their combined weekly food budget was $19 (£15). They were relying on packaged convenience foods. They would frequently run out of money and were becoming very aware of the impact that this food was having upon their health. So, I took them around their local market. We came home with carrier bags full of produce and we struggled to spend $12 (£10). I cooked them a simple curry from scratch that worked out at under a dollar per portion. It freezes beautifully, too, so I encouraged them to cook in larger batches so they could begin to fill their freezer with healthy "ready meals" instead.

Anyone can do the same. By simply eating more fresh whole foods, you will be taking in far more fiber, vitamins, minerals, trace elements, phytochemicals ... all the good stuff.

TAKE PROBIOTICS A FEW TIMES A YEAR

Probiotics, products that provide the good bacteria that live in the digestive tract, are a great way to give your digestive health a general boost. These bacteria regulate almost every aspect of digestion to one degree or another. Whether it is playing a role in the regulation of peristalsis (the rhythmical contraction of the digestive tract wall that moves everything along), through to repair and maintenance of tissues and structures within the digestive tract, they are massively important. That's why I think it's a good idea to give this bacterial colony a top off once in a while.

I generally say, if you are not directly trying to manage a specific digestive issue, then once every three months, take a course of probiotics. I recommend a broad-spectrum mixed culture probiotic (one with many different strains within it) to provide a broad range of these good bugs.

USEFUL RESOURCE

Viridian Nutrition
An extensive range of the cleanest supplements around. Over 180 products including vitamins, minerals, herbs, oils, and specific formulae made from the purest ingredients, with no additives, nasty fillers, or junk.
viridian-nutrition.com

RECIPES

Ginger, celery, and mint cooler I'm not overly obsessive with juicing, to be honest, but there are some ingredients that really can deliver a powerful punch when combined into a juice. This is a perfect example. The flavors are quite strong, but it is very effective.

MAKES 1 DRINK
3 celery stalks
leaves from a 1-oz (25-g) package of mint, plus a mint sprig for serving (optional)
¾- to 1¼-inch (2- to 3-cm) piece of ginger root

Run all the ingredients through a juicer and serve over crushed ice.

Serve with a mint sprig, if desired.

Pineapple and mint ice pops OK, for most of the year in some parts of the country, enjoying an ice pop is wishful thinking. But I have found these little treats a great delivery system for some wonderful ingredients that can offer benefit during an attack of the bloats.

MAKES 4
½ large pineapple, peeled, eyes, and any tough core removed, flesh chopped
⅔ cup (150 g) plain yogurt with active live cultures
5 drops of peppermint oil

Mix all the ingredients together in a blender, then blend into a smoothielike texture.

Pour this mixture into ice-pop molds and freeze overnight.

Tummy tea This lovely, settling tea can ease the symptoms of bloating quite rapidly. This effect comes from the essential oils that give the ingredients their distinctive flavors.

MAKES 1 DRINK
½ tsp caraway seeds
½ tsp fennel seeds
3 cardamom pods
6 mint leaves

Crush the seeds and the cardamom pods gently with the back of a spoon.

Place all the ingredients into a mug and top with boiled water. Let steep until the tea is beginning to cool, maybe 10 to 12 minutes, before drinking the tea.

Leek frittata As we saw in the introduction (see page 28), feeding the good bacteria in the digestive tract is an important part of long-term management of bloating, as well as of improving digestive function overall. The inulin in leeks feeds this good bacteria, enhancing its growth.

SERVES 1
1 small leek, sliced
2 tsp olive oil
sea salt
3 large eggs
1¾ oz (50 g) feta cheese

Preheat the broiler. In an ovenproof omelet pan, sauté the leek in the olive oil, along with a pinch of sea salt, until the leek softens.

Whisk the eggs in a bowl, then pour them over the leeks. Let cook over medium heat for three or four minutes, until the underside and outer edge have cooked, but most of the top and center are still raw.

Crumble over the feta, then place the pan under the broiler for another three minutes or so (keep your eye on it) until the frittata is fully cooked.

Greek salad with arugula and artichokes

I just adore a Greek salad. This twist on a classic adds ingredients that can help your body ease bloating using its own built-in mechanisms. Artichokes, arugula, and olives all aid in the production and release of bile. Bile is vital because it aids fat digestion and (importantly) is the body's own natural laxative. Constipation and impaired fat digestion can both cause or exacerbate bloating.

SERVES 1

For the dressing
2 Tbsp olive oil
2 tsp balsamic vinegar
½ tsp dried oregano
sea salt and freshly
    ground black pepper

For the salad
handful of mixed
    salad greens
2 handfuls of
    arugula leaves
2 Tbsp pitted
    kalamata olives
7 oz (200 g) cooked
    artichoke hearts
¼ cucumber, sliced
3½ oz (100 g) feta cheese

Mix all the dressing ingredients well and whisk them to create an emulsion.

Combine the greens, olives, artichoke hearts, cucumber, and dressing and toss well. Arrange on a serving plate and crumble the feta on top.

Jerusalem artichoke soup Let's start with a little warning. When you first try this soup you may think I have played an evil prank on you. Because initially it may feel like digestive warfare has unfolded and you will feel bloated and gassy afterward. But what you are experiencing is a massive feeding of the good bacteria which will cause the bacterial colony to grow and strengthen. The long-term benefit of this is that bloating will ease and many aspects of digestion and digestive health will improve. Another odd thing: these vegetables are not artichokes and have nothing to do with Jerusalem. Weird!

SERVES 1 TO 2

1 large white onion, minced
2 garlic cloves, minced
1 Tbsp olive oil
sea salt
1 lb 2 oz (500 g) Jerusalem artichokes, skin-on, chopped
generous 2 cups (500 ml) vegetable broth, plus more if needed
chili oil and red pepper flakes, for serving (optional)

In a large saucepan, sauté the onion and garlic in the olive oil, with a pinch of sea salt, until the onion softens. Add the Jerusalem artichokes and enough broth to cover. You can always add more if the soup is a little thick, but watery soup is just like gruel!

Simmer gently for around 20 minutes, until the artichokes have softened. Blend into a thick, smooth soup, adding more broth if you would like it thinner. Serve with a drizzle of chili oil and a sprinkle of red pepper flakes (if using).

Cardamom spiced yogurt parfait

I originally designed this exotic-tasting, refreshing dish to be a dessert, but it could easily make a fantastic and indulgent breakfast.

SERVES 1

½ tsp ground cardamom
1 tsp honey
⅔ cup (150 g) plain yogurt with active live cultures
1 Tbsp rolled oats
1 Tbsp blueberries
1 tsp flaxseeds

In a small bowl, mix the ground cardamom and honey into the yogurt.

Place the oats into a tall glass. Spoon half the yogurt on top of that, then add most of the blueberries. Top that with the remaining yogurt and sprinkle with the remaining blueberries and the flaxseeds.

Roasted red bell pepper houmous with crudités

This is so fresh and vibrant, with beautiful summery flavors, plus huge amounts of both soluble and insoluble fiber. Great to eat in the hot weather with a barbecue, or in the winter, dolloped on a baked sweet potato.

SERVES 2 FOR LUNCH

For the houmous
1 large red bell pepper, seeded and sliced lengthwise
drizzle of olive oil
sea salt
generous 1½ cups (400 g) canned chickpeas, drained and rinsed
1 garlic clove, minced
1 Tbsp tahini
juice of ½ lemon
2 Tbsp extra virgin olive oil

For the crudités
any combination of:
carrots, cucumbers, celery, fennel ...
whatever you desire

Preheat the oven to 400°F/200°C.

Place the sliced pepper on a baking sheet. Drizzle with olive oil, add a pinch of sea salt, and roast at the top of a hot oven for 20 to 25 minutes. Usually I advise that you turn peppers a few times during roasting, but here it is worth getting areas of charring to develop a deep flavor.

Put the chickpeas, garlic, tahini, roasted peppers, lemon juice, and extra virgin olive oil into a blender and blend to a smooth houmous.

Serve with the crudités.

Spinach dal I really am quite the fan of dal. Simple fare, yet very filling and packed with nutrients. Red lentils are packed with soluble fiber, which swells in the digestive tract and increases gut motility effectively. Great as a side dish with meat or fish, or just on its own.

SERVES 2

1 red onion, minced
3 garlic cloves, minced
1 Tbsp olive oil
1½ cups (250 g) red lentils
up to generous 2 cups
    (500 ml) vegetable
    broth (you may not
    need it all)
½ to 1 tsp mild curry
    powder, to taste
3 handfuls of
    baby spinach

Sauté the onion and garlic in the olive oil, until the onion has softened.

Add the lentils and a little of the vegetable broth and simmer. As the liquid starts to reduce, add more broth. Keep going like this until the lentils are soft and beginning to get broken down.

Add the curry powder and mix thoroughly.

Finally, keeping the dal on very low heat, add the spinach and stir until it begins to wilt.

Tuna steak with herbed bean salad

This is a gorgeous meal that is really a "dinner in minutes" job. When you want something quick but don't want to hit the junk food, this is ideal.

SERVES 1 GENEROUSLY

2½ cups (400 g) canned mixed beans, drained and rinsed
leaves from 1 small bunch of parsley, chopped
leaves from 1 small bunch of cilantro, chopped
sea salt and freshly ground black pepper
1 large tuna steak
2 Tbsp olive oil, plus 2 tsp for the tuna
juice of ½ lime, plus lime wedges for serving
½ tsp garlic powder or granules

Add the drained beans to a bowl with the chopped herbs and a pinch of sea salt and mix well, then set aside.

Lightly fry the tuna steak for three minutes on each side (slightly less if you like it seared) in the 2 tsp of olive oil.

Mix the lime juice, 2 Tbsp of olive oil, garlic powder, and salt and pepper to taste and whisk well to form a dressing. Dress the mixed beans and mix well once more.

Spoon the beans into the center of the plate and top with the tuna steak. Serve with lime wedges.

Bean and corn quesadillas I love quesadillas. Simple, gooey, delicious comfort food. Using wholewheat tortillas and wholesome fillings helps these to be really quite good for you, too.

SERVES 1

1¼ cups (200 g) canned mixed beans, drained and rinsed
2 Tbsp corn
½ small red or green chile, minced
leaves from a small bunch of cilantro, coarsely chopped
2 to 3 handfuls of grated cheddar cheese
sea salt and freshly ground black pepper
2 wholewheat tortillas

Preheat the oven to 400°F/200°C.

Place the beans in a bowl and partially mash them with a fork. Add the corn, chile, cilantro, and one handful of the grated cheddar, season with salt and pepper to taste, and mix well.

Spread the mixture over the top of one of the tortillas and sprinkle over the remaining cheese. Place the other tortilla on top, push down to tightly sandwich the two together, then place on a baking sheet and bake in the hot oven for 10 to 15 minutes, until the tortillas crisp up and begin to turn a golden brown.

Cut into quarters to serve.

Sweet potato, red lentil, and white bean miso stew This dish is fantastically filling. Sweet, warming, and hearty, it would make a perfect winter meal with some steamed greens. Miso is fermented soybean paste. It is super-nutritious and tastes amazing, too. It is available in most grocery and health food stores.

SERVES 2

1 large red onion, minced
2 garlic cloves, minced
sea salt and freshly ground black pepper
1 Tbsp olive oil
generous 1 cup (200 g) red lentils
1 medium sweet potato, skin-on, chopped
1 heaping Tbsp miso paste
1⅔ cups (400 g) canned lima beans, drained

Sauté the onion and garlic, along with a pinch of sea salt, in the oil until the onion is soft.

Add the lentils and sweet potato and enough water to almost cover the contents of the pan. Bring to a simmer. Add the miso paste and stir well until it has dissolved.

Continue simmering until the sweet potato has softened and the lentils are soft and semibroken down, creating a thick stew. Add the lima beans and mix well.

Season to taste if required, before serving with wilted greens.

Mediterranean barlotto

A barlotto is basically a risotto. But, instead of using the traditional arborio risotto rice (that is basically like glue in the digestive tract), it uses pearl barley. This is incredibly high in fiber and has a very low glycemic impact.

SERVES 2

1 large red onion, minced
2 garlic cloves, minced
1 Tbsp olive oil
sea salt
1⅓ cups (250 g) pearl barley
1 zucchini, cut into semicircular slices (a mixture of green and yellow if desired)
1 red bell pepper, seeded and chopped
8 to 10 sundried tomatoes, halved
4½ cups (1 liter) vegetable broth (plus more, if needed)
2 cups (400 g) canned chopped tomatoes

Begin by sautéing the onion and garlic in the olive oil, with a good pinch of sea salt, until the onion has softened.

Add the pearl barley and mix well. Keep stirring over medium heat for about a minute. Add the zucchini, pepper, and sundried tomatoes.

At this stage, begin adding small amounts of vegetable broth, bit by bit. Add a little, wait for it to be absorbed, then add a little more. Keep going like this until you have used around generous 2 cups (500 ml) of broth.

Add the canned tomatoes and continue to simmer until they have been absorbed, stirring the mixture frequently.

Taste the barlotto. If the barley is still a little firm, continue to add vegetable broth in small increments until the dish resembles a conventional risotto. Serve.

Baked sweet potato with white beans, spinach, and pesto

This is comfort food in my eyes. There is a wonderful satisfying, addictive quality about it. A perfect winter supper, with masses of fiber and—most importantly of all—masses of flavor!

SERVES 1

1 medium-size
   sweet potato
2 handfuls of
   baby spinach
1 Tbsp olive oil
1¼ cups (300 g) cooked
   lima beans (from a can
   is fine, drained
   and rinsed)
2 Tbsp pesto

Preheat the oven to 400°F/200°C.

Pierce the sweet potato using a knife or skewer, then place on a baking sheet and bake for an hour. OK, they take a while, but are *so* worth it!

Sauté the spinach in the olive oil, until it wilts. Stir in the beans and pesto. Mix well.

Split the baked sweet potato and top with the bean mixture. Easy peasy!

Ratatouille crumble

Ratatouille crumble This is amazing. I know, I would say that, but seriously. So much flavor. Great textures, huge amounts of fiber and an abundance of nutrients. Great with a side salad, or even in smaller portions as a side dish for white fish or chicken.

SERVES 1

1 large red onion, minced
2 garlic cloves, minced
1 Tbsp olive oil
sea salt and freshly ground black pepper
1 zucchini, cut into semicircular slices
1 red bell pepper, seeded and chopped
½ small eggplant, chopped
1¾ to generous 2 cups (400 to 500 g) strained tomatoes
handful or so of oats
2 Tbsp sunflower seeds
1 Tbsp flaxseeds
1 Tbsp grated Parmesan cheese

Begin by sautéing the onion and garlic in the oil, with a good pinch of sea salt, until the onion begins to soften. Add the zucchini, pepper, and eggplant and continue to sauté until all the vegetables are starting to get soft.

At this stage, add the strained tomatoes and a generous amount of salt and pepper (to taste) and simmer for 12 to 15 minutes, stirring frequently. The mixture needs to reduce to a thick ratatouille, not vegetables in a watery tomato sauce. Give it enough time to reduce and thicken. Meanwhile, preheat the oven to 350°F/180°C.

Transfer the mixture to a baking dish. Sprinkle enough oats over the top to give an even coverage of about ¼ in (5 mm) thickness. Dishes vary, that's why I don't specify a measurement, just sprinkle it evenly and you are away! Sprinkle the seeds and Parmesan over the top. Bake in the oven for 10 to 12 minutes, long enough for the crumble topping to turn golden and crispy.

Easy vegetable curry with herbed quinoa

This is a great basic curry recipe. Using bought curry powder may be culinary heresy but, if you are new to making curries, it is a fast-track way to cooking them yourself. Use any combination of vegetables you desire.

SERVES 2

For the curry
1 large red onion,
    minced
3 garlic cloves, minced
1 Tbsp olive oil
sea salt and freshly
    ground black pepper
1 zucchini, sliced
½ small eggplant,
    finely chopped
1 Tbsp curry powder
    of your choice
1 Tbsp tomato paste
1 cup (200 g) canned
    chopped tomatoes
2 handfuls of
    baby spinach

For the quinoa
½ cup (100 g) quinoa
large bunch of cilantro,
    coarsely chopped
juice of ½ lime

Sauté the onion and garlic in the oil, with a good pinch of salt, until the onion begins to soften.

Add the zucchini and eggplant and continue to sauté for another five minutes, until the vegetables begin to soften.

Add the curry powder, tomato paste, and canned tomatoes and simmer gently for around 20 minutes. If you find the curry starting to look a little dry, add small splashes of water to top off the sauce. Remember, only in small amounts, and keep tasting to check the seasoning.

At the last minute, add the baby spinach and keep stirring until it wilts.

Meanwhile, simmer the quinoa in water for around 20 minutes, until the quinoa has enlarged, softened, and what looks like little tails form at the sides. Drain. Mix with the cilantro, lime juice, and salt and pepper to taste.

Seafood brown rice with lemon grass and cilantro

This is a lovely, delicately flavored dish that packs a huge fiber punch and has a wonderful flavor. It is great on its own, or with a side of stir-fried vegetables, or even a salad.

SERVES 2

2 large lemon grass stalks
¾ cup (150 g) short-grain brown rice
2 garlic cloves, minced
¾-in (2-cm) ginger root, peeled and minced
3 scallions, cut lengthwise into long strips
a little olive oil
sea salt
7 oz (200 g) cooked mixed seafood
2 tsp soy sauce
small bunch of cilantro
juice of ¼ lime

Bash the lemon grass stalks with something heavy, such as a rolling pin, to split and bruise them so the juices easily flow out. Cut in half and place, with the brown rice, in a saucepan. Add enough water to just cover, then bring to a boil. Simmer for 30 to 35 minutes, until the rice is soft. The most important thing is that you do not add loads of water at once. Keep topping off the water as the rice looks dry. This way the flavor of the lemon grass will infuse into the rice, rather than into a load of water that will be thrown away. When the rice has cooked, simmer until only the smallest amount of water remains, stirring to stop the rice sticking and catching.

In a wok or large frying pan, cook the garlic, ginger, and scallions in a dash of oil, with a good pinch of sea salt, until the garlic begins to mellow in aroma, stirring constantly. Add the seafood and stir-fry for about three minutes.

Add the brown rice, discarding the lemon grass, and mix well. Add the soy sauce, cilantro, and lime juice and mix thoroughly before serving.

Pea and asparagus brown rice risotto

This simple risotto is full of flavor, full of fiber, and can look rather impressive, too. If you want to make a simpler version, then leave out the puree-making process. Brown rice risotto needs a greater amount of broth than regular risotto.

SERVES 2

1 large onion, minced (keep about 1 Tbsp aside)

3 garlic cloves, minced (keep 1 chopped clove aside)

1 Tbsp olive oil, plus 2 tsp sea salt

1⅓ cups (250 g) short-grain brown rice

4½ cups (1 liter) vegetable broth, plus more if needed

2 cups (250 g) frozen peas (set aside ½ cup/70 g)

4¼ oz (120 g) asparagus spears, halved

Sauté the onion and garlic (apart from that you have set aside) in the 1 Tbsp of oil with a pinch of salt, until the onion is soft.

Add the brown rice and 4 to 5 Tbsp of broth. Simmer until the stock looks like it has almost completely absorbed. Then add a little more.

Keep adding the broth little and often, cooking for around 45 minutes, until a thick risotto texture has formed. You may even need some more broth, as brown rice can be demanding!

Halfway through the process, add the peas. During the last five minutes, add the asparagus.

Meanwhile, in a separate pan, sauté the reserved onion and garlic with some sea salt in the 2 tsp of oil until the onion has softened. Add the remaining peas and just enough vegetable broth to cover. Simmer until the peas are soft, then blend to a smooth puree.

Portion the risotto into bowls and create a small well in the center of each. Fill with the puree.

Beet, goat cheese, and arugula tortilla pizza

This is a perfect shortcut quick-fix type affair. I like a tortilla pizza, as you get the same kind of pizza fix, but you don't have about 8 in (20 cm) of pure refined starch on your plate. The tortilla is so thin that it is little more than a carrier for other amazing ingredients.

SERVES 1

2 tsp tomato paste
1 large wholewheat tortilla
1 large or 2 small cooked beet, chopped
2½ oz (70 g) goat cheese
1 Tbsp pine nuts
handful of arugula leaves

Preheat the broiler to its highest setting.

Spread the tomato paste over one side of the tortilla. Top with the beet. Crumble over the goat cheese and sprinkle with the pine nuts.

Place under the hot broiler until the cheese is bubbling and beginning to brown on the edges.

Place on a plate, then top with the arugula.

Eggplant layer bake This is such a lovely hearty dish that evokes memories of Mediterranean vacations ... ah, and it's pretty good for you too!

SERVES 2 TO 3

3 large eggplants, sliced lengthwise
1 Tbsp olive oil
1 large red onion, minced
2 garlic cloves, minced
½ red bell pepper, seeded and chopped
sea salt and freshly ground black pepper
3 cups (680 g) strained tomatoes
2 tsp dried basil
6 cups (300 g) baby spinach
handful of grated mozzarella (optional)

Preheat the oven to 400°F/200°C.

Begin by lightly frying (or griddling, if you want griddle marks) the eggplant slices in a small amount of olive oil, until they soften. This improves the texture of the dish in the long run.

Sauté the onion, garlic, and red pepper in the remaining olive oil with a good pinch of sea salt, until the onion and pepper have softened.

Add the strained tomatoes and dried basil and simmer for about 15 minutes, until the tomatoes thicken slightly. Season with salt and pepper. Stir in the baby spinach until it wilts.

Line a deep baking dish with some of the eggplant slices. Top with a layer of the strained tomato mixture. Then top with another layer of eggplant slices, then strained tomato, then eggplant. Keep repeating this process.

Place the baking dish at the top of a hot oven, and bake for about 40 minutes, until the eggplant is fully cooked and the sauce has reduced. Top with mozzarella and return to the oven just long enough for the cheese to melt.

Date, almond, and chia balls

Chia seeds seem to be quite the popular ingredient at the moment. While it is fair to say that some of the claims people are making for them are really rather daft, they are an indisputably wonderful source of soluble fiber.

MAKES 25
scant 1 cups (250 g) pitted dates
2 cups (250 g) raw almonds
3 tsp chia seeds
dry unsweetened coconut, for coating

Place the dates, most of the almonds, and chia seeds into a food processor and blitz on the highest setting until a stiff paste forms. Add the remaining almonds and blitz briefly, so there are some big chunks of nut in the paste.

Sprinkle the dry unsweetened coconut onto a plate. Processing the ingredients at such high speed will have squeezed all of the oil from the almonds, so the paste will be very oily. Break off thumb-size pieces of paste, roll into balls, then roll them in the coconut. Place the coated balls on a clean plate.

Once all of the paste has been rolled into balls, place them into the refrigerator for several hours, which will make them firmer and give them a great chewy texture.

Date squares These are such a wonderful snack, perfect with a nice cup of tea! Packed with fiber, iron, and B vitamins, plus they satisfy the sweet treat craving. What a bargain!

MAKES 6 TO 8

¾ cup (150 g) coconut oil, plus more for the pan
1½ cups (200 g) pitted dates, chopped
3 Tbsp honey
¾ cup (75 g) rolled oats
1½ cups (200 g) wholewheat flour
3 Tbsp mixed seeds

Oil a 9-in (23-cm) baking pan with coconut oil. Preheat the oven to 350°F/180°C.

Place the dates into a saucepan with 2 Tbsp of water. Heat the pan and cook the dates down to a gooey paste. In another pan, melt the honey and coconut oil together.

In a bowl, mix the oats, flour, and mixed seeds. Pour in the melted honey mixture and stir well to form a dough.

Spoon half the dough into the prepared pan, pushing down firmly. Top with the date mixture, then spread the remaining dough over that.

Bake in the oven for around 30 minutes, or until the top has turned a golden brown.

Let cool completely in the pan before cutting into six to eight squares.

Figgy seeded flapjacks
Figs in flapjacks just give a real texture treat. From chewy, to crunchy, to sticky. A great combination.

MAKES 6 TO 8

scant 1 cup (140 g) chopped soft dried figs
scant ½ cup (80 g) coconut oil
6 Tbsp honey
generous 3⅛ cups (300 g) rolled oats
scant ½ cup (50 g) goji berries
⅓ cup (50 g) pitted dates, chopped
½ cup (75 g) mixed seeds

Preheat the oven to 375°F/190°C. Line a 9-in (23-cm) baking pan with baking parchment.

Place the figs in a saucepan with about ⅔ cup (150 ml) of water and simmer until the water has reduced by half. Transfer to a food processor and blend into a paste.

Melt the coconut oil and honey together in a pan. Add the fig paste and combine well.

Add the fig mixture to the remaining ingredients in a bowl and mix well.

Transfer the mixture to the prepared baking pan and bake for about 25 minutes, until they begin to turn golden. Let cool completely in the pan before cutting into six to eight squares.

Apple oat crumble

Apple oat crumble I am very partial to a nice apple crumble. Unfortunately, many versions of this lovely dessert are overly packed with sugar, which really isn't necessary. This version is a much healthier option.

SERVES 2

For the filling
15¾ oz (450 g) apples, skin-on, cored and chopped
¼ tsp stevia
1 tsp ground cinnamon

For the crumble
¾ cup (100 g) wholewheat flour
scant 1 cup (87 g) rolled oats
¼ tsp stevia
1 Tbsp mixed seeds
scant ½ cup (85 g) coconut oil

Preheat the oven to 350°F/180°C.

Start with the filling. Place the apples and stevia in a saucepan with 1 Tbsp of water and simmer over high heat for 10 to 12 minutes, until the apples are soft and beginning to stew. Add the cinnamon and mix well. Remove from the heat and spoon into a 9-in (23-cm) ovenproof dish, or into two individual ovenproof bowls.

Mix the flour, oats, stevia, and mixed seeds together. Melt the coconut oil and stir it into the oat mixture. Sprinkle the crumble mixture over the apples, pressing down gently.

Bake in the oven for 15 to 20 minutes, long enough for the crumble to start to get crunchy and the apples to start bubbling away nicely.

Mediterranean scramble A quick, filling and flavorsome breakfast.

SERVES 1
1 plum tomato,
   chopped
2 tsp olive oil
2 large eggs,
   lightly beaten
2½ oz (70 g) feta cheese
small sprig of basil,
   coarsely chopped

Sauté the tomato in the olive oil for seven or eight minutes. Add the eggs and keep stirring until a scrambled egg has formed.

Crumble over the feta cheese and basil.

Salmon kedgeree I am quite a fan of kedgeree. It can keep you full for hours and really set you up for a busy day.

SERVES 1 TO 2
generous ⅓ cup (75 g)
   brown basmati rice
½ tsp curry powder
handful of baby spinach
sea salt and freshly
   ground black pepper
1 cooked salmon fillet,
   skinned and broken
   into pieces
2 large hard-cooked
   eggs, cut into wedges

Place the rice and curry powder into a saucepan, top with enough water to cover, and simmer over high heat for around 20 minutes, until the rice has softened. You may need to top off the water now and then during the cooking time.

At the last minute, stir through the baby spinach to wilt. Taste and adjust the seasoning.

Once the rice is cooked, stir in the flaked salmon and mix well.

Plate the rice mixture and place the egg wedges on top.

Cinnamon oatmeal with oat milk

Some grains can be problematic when following a FODMAP diet, but oats are no problem. This lovely warming oatmeal is ready in minutes.

SERVES 1

½ cup (50 g) rolled oats
scant 1 cup (225 ml) oat milk
1 tsp ground cinnamon
2 tsp maple syrup

Place the oats and oat milk in a pan and simmer for five to six minutes, or until the oats soften.

Add the cinnamon and serve, drizzled with the maple syrup. Add blueberries and strawberries in season, for a fruity treat.

Roasted squash soup

Roasted squash soup Slow-roasting the squash in this recipe gives a nice depth of flavor. As you will be avoiding onions and garlic on FODMAP, creating this greater depth of flavor is really important.

SERVES 2 TO 3

1 large butternut squash, skin-on, chopped
1 Tbsp olive oil
sea salt and freshly ground black pepper
1¾ cups (400 g) canned coconut milk
scant 1 cup (200 ml) vegetable broth
sesame seeds and cilantro sprigs, for serving (optional)

Preheat the oven to 400°F/200°C.

Place the squash in a roasting pan. Drizzle with olive oil and add a generous pinch of sea salt and pepper, toss well, then roast at the top of the hot oven for around 45 minutes. Turn occasionally, but I do like to let some of the edges brown and caramelize slightly, as this gives great flavor.

Once roasted, transfer the squash to a saucepan. Add the coconut milk and enough broth to cover. Season with a little more salt and pepper and simmer for 10 minutes.

Transfer to a blender or food processor and blend into a thick, luscious soup. Serve with a sprinkle of sesame and cilantro (if using).

Turkey-stuffed red bell peppers

This is a gorgeous dish and great all year round. Try it with a big fresh salad in the summer, or with cooked veg on the side in the winter. Filling, tasty, and fresh.

SERVES 1

scant 1 cup (200 g)
   ground turkey
1 egg, lightly beaten
1 Tbsp pitted, chopped
   kalamata olives
2 tsp dried oregano
sea salt and freshly
   ground black pepper
2 red bell peppers, halved
   and seeded
4 to 8 tsp grated
   Parmesan cheese,
   to taste

Preheat the oven to 350°F/180°C.

Mix the turkey, egg, olives, oregano, and generous amounts of salt and pepper together.

Stuff this mixture into the four pepper halves, then top each with 1 to 2 tsp of grated Parmesan.

Bake in the oven for 50 minutes. Serve with a side salad or cooked vegetables.

Grilled halloumi with Mediterranean roasted vegetables and quinoa Just a pure taste of summer. Filling yet light. My idea of heaven.

SERVES 1
scant ½ cup (75 g) quinoa
1 red bell pepper, seeded
   and chopped
½ zucchini, sliced
1 to 2 Tbsp olive oil,
   plus 2 tsp
1 tsp dried oregano
½ tsp garlic granules
¼ tsp smoked paprika
sea salt and freshly
   ground black pepper
3 to 4 slices of halloumi
   cheese

Preheat the oven to 350°F/180°C.

Place the quinoa in a pan and cover with boiling water. Simmer for 20 minutes, until it is soft and small tail-like projections form at the side of each grain. Drain.

Meanwhile, combine the vegetables with the 1 to 2 Tbsp of olive oil, the dried oregano, garlic granules, and smoked paprika, along with a good pinch of salt and pepper. Mix well, then place in a roasting pan and roast in the oven for 20 to 25 minutes, stirring frequently.

In a griddle pan or small frying pan, gently fry the halloumi in the 2 tsp of olive oil for three or four minutes maximum each side. You want to do it for just long enough for the halloumi to begin to turn a golden brown on each side.

Serve the quinoa on a plate with the roasted veg and top with the halloumi.

Chicken and spinach miso rice bowl

This is a lovely comforting dish that is a little like a Chinese congee, but with the satisfying flavors of Japanese miso soup.

SERVES 1

1 large chicken breast
generous ⅓ cup (75 g) brown rice
1 Tbsp miso paste (any will do, but ideally brown if you have it)
2 handfuls of baby spinach

Preheat the oven to 375°F/190°C.

Place the chicken breast on a baking sheet and roast for about 30 minutes.

Meanwhile, cover the rice in boiling water and simmer gently for about 20 minutes, until the rice is soft, then drain.

Pour about 1½ mugs of hot water into a bowl. Add the miso paste and stir until dissolved.

Add the rice to the center of the bowl, trying to make a mound amid the soup.

Place the baby spinach leaves on top so they wilt naturally. Slice the chicken breast and lay the slices on top of the spinach.

Stir-fried satay greens with brown rice

This dish is deceptively simple-sounding. I have modified my regular version that uses garlic and onions. This is a full-flavored way to make the most of green vegetables that are often rather dull, and a taste sensation that it is easy to get hooked on.

SERVES 1

generous ⅓ cup (75 g) brown rice
1 large head of collard greens, shredded
1 zucchini, sliced
1 Tbsp olive oil
sea salt and freshly ground black pepper
1 heaping Tbsp peanut butter (a decent no-added-sugar variety)
2 tsp soy sauce
1 tsp maple syrup
½ tsp Chinese 5-spice

Place the rice in a saucepan, cover with boiling water, and simmer for 20 minutes, until soft.

Meanwhile, sauté the greens and zucchini in the olive oil, along with a good pinch of sea salt, until the zucchini has softened. Keep them moving the whole time as they can sometimes catch and burn, leaving a bitter flavor.

Stir in the peanut butter, soy sauce, and maple syrup and mix well. Sprinkle over the 5-spice and mix well again.

Serve with the brown rice.

Yaki soba Having been fortunate enough to spend a lot of time in Japan, I really developed a love for soba noodles. These are made from buckwheat, a very nutrient-dense grain that is gentle on the digestion. Be sure to get the true buckwheat version as these will be fine for FODMAP (some contain wheat, which is not).

SERVES 1

1 small carrot, cut into thin sticks
1 small zucchini, cut into thin sticks
1 Tbsp olive oil
3½ oz (100 g) raw king shrimp, shelled, deveined if necessary
4-oz (114-g) portion of soba noodles (these are often preportioned in the packages)
2 tsp soy sauce
2 tsp sesame oil
sea salt

In a wok or large frying pan, stir-fry the carrot and zucchini in the oil for about 10 minutes, until they begin to soften. Add the king shrimp and continue to stir-fry for another three minutes or so, until the shrimp are cooked.

Meanwhile, put the soba noodles in a saucepan, pour over boiling water, and simmer for around 10 minutes, until soft. Drain.

Add the noodles to the vegetables and shrimp and toss together well. Add the soy sauce and sesame oil, with a pinch of sea salt, and toss well.

Spiced quinoa with shredded spinach, dill, feta, and kalamata olives

This is bursting with flavor and has a lovely Greek vibe going on. This is great as a side dish with white fish or chicken, or as a lunchtime salad.

SERVES 1

scant ½ cup (75 g) quinoa
½ small cucumber, chopped
2 handfuls of baby spinach, shredded
2 Tbsp pitted kalamata olives, chopped
½ cup (80 g) crumbled feta cheese
small bunch of fresh dill, coarsely chopped
½ tsp ground cinnamon
sea salt and freshly ground black pepper

Place the quinoa in a saucepan and cover with boiling water. Simmer for around 20 minutes, until the grain has softened and a small tail-like projection appears on the side of each. Drain.

In a bowl, mix the quinoa, cucumber, spinach, olives, feta, and dill together and toss well.

Sprinkle over the cinnamon, plus a little salt and some black pepper, and mix well before serving.

Chicken and shiitake pad thai

I do love a good pad thai. Unfortunately the conventional recipe contains quite a few FODMAPs. This little rejigging has created a version that is close to the real thing, but won't cause you problems later on. Winner!

SERVES 1

4¼ oz (125 g) flat rice noodles
1 red chile, minced, seeds left in
1 Tbsp olive oil
1 skinless chicken breast, chopped
1 cup (75 g) sliced shiitake mushrooms
juice of 1 lime
2 tsp fish sauce
2 tsp soy sauce
2 tsp agave or maple syrup
handful of salted peanuts
small bunch of cilantro, coarsely chopped

Place the rice noodles in a bowl and cover with hot water. Let soften (around 15 minutes, but check the package).

In a wok or large pan, stir-fry the chile in the olive oil for about a minute.

Add the chicken and continue to stir-fry for eight minutes or so, until the chicken is cooked. If in doubt, cut a piece in half. If there is any trace of pink, continue to stir-fry for a minute, then check again.

Add the shiitake mushrooms and continue to stir-fry until they have cooked.

Drain the softened noodles, then add to the pan, mix well, and reduce the heat.

Add the lime juice, fish sauce, soy sauce, and agave or maple syrup and mix thoroughly. Plate up and sprinkle with the peanuts and cilantro.

Chicken, red bell pepper, and olive tray bake

This simple one-dish recipe is great come rain or shine. Bursting with Mediterranean flavor and bundles of nutrients.

SERVES 2

2 full chicken legs (drumsticks and thighs attached)
2 large red bell peppers, seeded and sliced lengthwise
1 Tbsp olive oil
1 Tbsp balsamic vinegar
1 tsp dried basil
3 bay leaves
sea salt and freshly ground black pepper
1 Tbsp pitted kalamata olives

Preheat the oven to 375°F/190°C.

Place the chicken and peppers in a baking dish. Top with the olive oil and balsamic vinegar and toss well. Sprinkle over the dried basil, scrunch up the bay leaves, and throw them in, season, then place the dish at the top of the hot oven and bake for 45 minutes, stirring once. Drop in the olives when there are five minutes to go.

Serve with a side salad, or some cooked quinoa.

Turkey meatballs with sautéed zucchini and roasted sweet potato

This is a little more time-consuming, but great as a weekend feel-good meal. Super-filling and flavorsome.

SERVES 2

1⅓ cups (300 g) ground turkey
1 egg, lightly beaten
2 tsp dried mixed herbs
1 tsp grated Parmesan
¼ zucchini, grated, plus 1 zucchini, sliced
sea salt and freshly ground black pepper
1 small sweet potato, cut into wedges
2 Tbsp olive oil, plus more for the sweet potatoes
¾ cup (180 ml) chicken broth

Preheat the oven to 375°F/190°C.

Place the turkey, egg, mixed herbs, Parmesan, and grated zucchini into a bowl, with a good pinch of salt and some pepper. Mix well, then roll into meatballs about 1 in (2.5 cm) in size. Place on a plate and chill for 30 minutes. This gives you a little more firmness to work with.

Place the sweet potato wedges on a baking sheet, drizzle with olive oil and a pinch of salt, mix well, and bake for 25 to 30 minutes, or until the sweet potato is soft, the edges are crisp, and golden. Make sure you turn them often.

In a pan with a lid, fry the meatballs in 1 Tbsp of the olive oil for about seven minutes, turning often, until they begin to turn a golden brown.

Add two-thirds of the chicken broth, cover, and cook until most of the liquid has been absorbed. Add the remaining liquid and cook, uncovered, until all the liquid has gone.

When they are nearly ready, sauté the sliced zucchini in the remaining oil with plenty of sea salt and black pepper, until the zucchini is soft.

Stuffed chicken with pesto vegetables

The FODMAPs diet can sometimes leave people feeling a little bit bored, as when they first see the list of dietary restrictions it can make their heart sink. This dish goes to show that this doesn't need to be the case. Garlic-free pesto is found in health food stores.

SERVES 2

1 large zucchini, sliced
1 large red bell pepper, seeded and sliced lengthwise
½ small eggplant, chopped
1 Tbsp olive oil
1 Tbsp garlic-free pesto
2 large skin-on chicken breasts
5 cups (250 g) baby spinach
1 Tbsp ricotta cheese
generous 1 cup (10 g) dill weed, coarsely chopped
freshly ground black pepper
1¾ oz (50 g) feta cheese

Preheat the oven to 400°F/200°C.

Sauté the zucchini, pepper, and eggplant in a little olive oil, until all the vegetables have softened. Add the pesto and mix well.

Meanwhile, take the chicken breasts and slowly run fingers along the inside of the skin, to separate it from the flesh and create a pocket.

Place the spinach in a steamer for four to five minutes, until wilting. Squeeze all moisture out of it, then finely chop. Transfer the spinach to a bowl with the ricotta and dill, along with some black pepper, and mix well. Crumble over the feta cheese and gently mix again.

Fill the space between the skin and breast with the spinach and feta mix. Place the chicken breasts on a roasting tray and roast at the top of a hot oven for around 20 minutes. Serve with the zucchini mixture.

Mango cantaloupe chia smoothie

This unusual-but-tasty smoothie has a fabulous texture, thanks to the chia seeds. These little shots of omega-3 help to increase the anti-inflammatory punch already delivered by the carotenoids in the fruits. This smoothie does come out quite thick, so you could easily transfer it to a bowl and top with seeds and chopped fruits as a dessert or breakfast.

MAKES 1

1 mango, peeled and pitted
¼ cantaloupe melon, peeled and seeded
⅔ cup (150 g) plain yogurt with active live cultures
1 Tbsp chia seeds

Place all the ingredients into a blender and blend into a thick smoothie.

Roasted squash, carrot, and ginger soup

This is so warming and lovely. A perfect winter treat. It is also a great base for a curry if you find you have leftovers. Packed with carotenoids and anti-inflammatory gingerols.

SERVES 2 TO 3

4 large carrots,
    skin-on, chopped
½ large squash,
    skin-on, chopped
1½ Tbsp olive oil
sea salt
1 large red onion,
    minced
2 garlic cloves, minced
1-inch (2.5-cm) ginger
    root, peeled and
    minced
generous 2 cups (500 ml)
    vegetable broth (you
    may not need it all)
pumpkin seeds and
    slivered red bell pepper,
    for seving (optional)

Preheat the oven to 375°F/190°C.

Place the carrots and squash on a roasting tray, drizzle with ½ Tbsp of the olive oil and a pinch of sea salt, and roast for around 30 minutes, until soft and the edges are beginning to caramelize.

In a large saucepan, sauté the onion, garlic, and ginger in the remaining 1 Tbsp of olive oil, with a good pinch of sea salt, until the onion softens.

Transfer the roasted carrots and squash to the pan with the onion and garlic and pour in enough broth to just cover the vegetables. Simmer for five minutes, then transfer to a blender or food processor and blend into a smooth soup. Serve sprinkled with pumpkin seeds and red bell pepper, if desired.

Pineapple coconut smoothie This is super-refreshing, filling, and packed with the anti-inflammatory enzyme bromelain.

**MAKES 1 LARGE OR
2 SMALL SMOOTHIES**
½ large pineapple,
    peeled, eyes removed
1¾ cups (400 g) canned
    coconut milk
¼ tsp turmeric

Place all the ingredients into a blender and blend into a thick, luscious smoothie.

Spaghetti with red bell peppers, anchovies, and capers
Simple, wholesome, feel-good food. This is perfect for a lazy weekend, or one of those moments when you want something simple but satisfying.

SERVES 1

2¼ oz (60 g) wholewheat spaghetti
½ red onion, sliced
1 Tbsp olive oil
sea salt and freshly ground black pepper
1 red bell pepper, seeded and finely chopped
1 small (1¾oz/50 g) can of anchovy fillets (retain the oil)
½ tsp capers, drained and rinsed
finely grated Parmesan, for serving

Place the spaghetti in a pan and cover with boiling water. Simmer until the pasta is cooked al dente (check the package directions).

Sauté the onion in the olive oil, with a pinch of sea salt, until it has softened.

Add the red bell pepper and continue to sauté for another five to seven minutes, until the pepper is soft, too.

Add the drained spaghetti, the anchovies and their oil, and the capers and toss well until all the ingredients are well combined.

Put into a serving bowl, then add Parmesan and black pepper to taste.

Roasted salmon with spiced squash puree

This is a lovely looking dish, with deep, warming flavors and good amounts of that all-important anti-inflammatory omega-3.

SERVES 1

1 tsp sesame oil
2 tsp soy sauce
1 tsp honey
1 large salmon fillet
½ medium butternut squash, skin-on, chopped
2 tsp olive oil
sea salt and freshly ground black pepper
1 tsp ground cinnamon
pea shoots, for serving (optional)

Preheat the oven to 375°F/190°C.

Mix the sesame oil, soy sauce, and honey to make a marinade. Marinate the salmon in it for 30 minutes, turning once if you can.

Place the squash into a roasting tray, drizzle with olive oil and a pinch of salt and pepper, and roast for around 40 minutes, turning occasionally.

Transfer the roasted squash to a food processor. Add 3 Tbsp of water and sprinkle the cinnamon over. Blend to a smooth puree.

Meanwhile, place the marinated salmon on a baking sheet and pour the remaining marinade over the top of it. Bake for around 20 minutes, until lightly cooked and the marinade is beginning to caramelize slightly.

Spread a generous amount of the squash puree in the center of the plate and place the salmon fillet on top. Serve with a sprinkle of pea shoots (if using).

Tuna and red bell pepper kebabs with spinach and apricot salad

These are a bit special. Fresh tuna steak can be pricey, but as a treat it is a great ingredient. It is a fantastic source of omega-3 fatty acids and also of the mineral selenium.

SERVES 1

1 large tuna steak,
   cut into cubes
½ red bell pepper, seeded
   and cut into squares
sea salt and freshly
   ground black pepper
2 handfuls of
   baby spinach
4 to 5 dried apricots,
   halved

For the dressing
2 Tbsp extra virgin
   olive oil
1 tsp balsamic vinegar
½ tsp honey
¼ tsp ground cumin

Soak two wooden skewers in water for 30 minutes, so they don't burn under the broiler. Preheat the broiler to the highest setting.

Divide the tuna and red bell pepper across the drained skewers, arranging them alternately. Season with salt and pepper, then lay on a foil-lined baking sheet and place under the hot broiler. Broil for six to seven minutes, turning frequently. (Or less if you want the fish pinker.)

Combine the spinach and apricots. Separately whisk the dressing ingredients together to emulsify. Dress the salad and toss well.

Place the salad in the center of the serving plate and lay the skewers crisscross over it.

Avocado, smoked salmon, and spinach wrap with citrus mayo

This is great portable lunch that is much lighter than the usual "house brick" sandwiches available. Packed with omega-3, iron, and B vitamins.

MAKES 1

2 Tbsp mayonnaise
juice of ½ lemon
freshly ground
    black pepper
1 large wholewheat
    tortilla wrap
3 to 4 slices of
    smoked salmon
½ avocado, peeled
    and sliced
handful of baby spinach

Mix the mayonnaise with the lemon juice and a little black pepper and set aside.

Lay the tortilla wrap out and top with the smoked salmon and avocado.

Spread over the lemon mayonnaise, then finish the wrap by adding the baby spinach, before rolling it tightly. Eat!

Spinach and sweet potato curry

The beauty of this dish is that not only is it a super-easy curry to make, it is also packed with powerful anti-inflammatory compounds and prebiotic components, too.

SERVES 2

1 Tbsp olive oil
2 red onions, thinly sliced
2 large garlic cloves, minced
1 tsp grated ginger root
2 green chiles, finely sliced
1 tsp ground coriander
1 tsp ground cumin
1 tsp black mustard seeds
1 heaping tsp turmeric
1¾ lb (800 g) sweet potato, skin-on, chopped
1½ cups (375 ml) vegetable broth
2½ cups (150 g) coarsely chopped spinach
large handful of cilantro leaves, coarsely torn
1 Tbsp toasted slivered almonds
1 Tbsp dry unsweetened coconut

Heat the olive oil in a large saucepan and cook the onions, garlic, ginger, and chiles. When the onions have softened, add all the spices and heat until they are becoming fragrant.

Add the sweet potato and broth and simmer for 15 to 20 minutes, until the sweet potato is soft.

At this point, add the spinach. Once the spinach has wilted, the curry is ready to serve with cilantro leaves, topped with the slivered almonds, and sprinkled with the coconut.

Roasted chicken breast with pineapple salsa on spiced vegetables

This dish brings together several powerful anti-inflammatory ingredients into one simple, quick evening meal. You can now buy fresh pineapple prepared in small packages, which saves on time and waste.

SERVES 1

1 large chicken breast
generous ¾ cup (120 g) finely chopped fresh pineapple
1 scallion, minced
sea salt and freshly ground black pepper
1 large red onion, halved, then sliced
1¼-in (3-cm) ginger root, peeled and minced
2 garlic cloves, minced
1 Tbsp olive oil
1 large zucchini, sliced
2 handfuls of baby spinach
¼ tsp ground cumin
¼ tsp turmeric
¼ tsp curry powder
¼ tsp ground cinnamon

Preheat the oven to 400°F/200°C. Place the chicken breast on a baking sheet and bake for 20 minutes.

Meanwhile, combine the pineapple and scallion, add a little black pepper, and mix well.

Sauté the onion, ginger, and garlic with a pinch of sea salt in the olive oil until the onion has softened. Add the zucchini and continue to sauté for five to eight minutes, until the zucchini is soft.

Add the baby spinach and the spices. Mix well and sauté until the spinach wilts.

Place the vegetables in the center of the serving plate, top with the chicken breast, then add a generous helping of the pineapple salsa on top.

Spiced chicken meatloaf with roasted roots

I do love a meatloaf, but if you are dealing with inflammatory issues I'd keep red meat intake down a bit so as to reduce arachidonic acid intake. Chicken is a wonderful alternative and lends itself well to these spices.

SERVES 4

14 oz (400 g) skinless
  chicken breast
1 egg, lightly beaten
½ lemon grass stalk
  (the soft, lighter parts
  only), minced
small bunch of cilantro,
  coarsely chopped
2 scallions, minced
1 Tbsp sweet chili sauce
1 tsp turmeric
sea salt and freshly
  ground black pepper
unsalted butter, for the
  pan

Preheat the oven to 350°F/180°C.

Place the chicken breast into a food processor and process into ground meat. Mix the ground chicken with the rest of the ingredients, plus a generous pinch of salt and pepper.

Press the mixture into a buttered medium-size loaf pan and bake for around 40 minutes.

Serve with a side salad, or stir-fried greens.

Herbed salmon burgers with avocado salsa and spinach-strawberry balsamic salad

This may sound like a really peculiar combination, but I stumbled on it quite by accident ... well, using up leftovers to be precise. Give it a try and you will see what a delight it is.

SERVES 2

½ avocado, peeled
3 plum tomatoes
½ red chile
sea salt and freshly ground black pepper
2 skinless salmon fillets, chopped
1 garlic clove, minced
1 Tbsp chopped parsley leaves
1 Tbsp chopped cilantro leaves
1 Tbsp olive oil, plus 2 tsp
1 tsp balsamic vinegar
handful of baby spinach
6 to 7 strawberries, halved

Make the salsa by chopping the avocado, plum tomatoes, and chile. Combine these ingredients with a little black pepper.

Place the salmon fillets, garlic, herbs, and a pinch of sea salt into a food processor and process into a smooth ground texture.

Remove the mixture, divide into two, and form each into a burger patty shape.

Gently fry these burgers for about five minutes on each side in the 2 tsp of olive oil, until turning a golden color.

Mix the remaining 1 Tbsp of olive oil and the balsamic vinegar and whisk into a dressing.

Place the spinach on the plate, dot the strawberries over the leaves, and dress with the balsamic dressing.

Place the salmon burgers on top, then top the burgers with the avocado salsa.

INDEX

Clare Hulton—we are really cooking on gas now! Amazing work.
Thank you! Jenny Liddle—you are tireless at what you do! Tanya
Murkett—as always, supporting me and putting up with me no
matter what! A big thank you to all the team at Quadrille, Smith &
Gilmour, Martin Poole, and Aya Nishimura. Catherine Tyldesley,
Gaby Roslin, and all of the wonderful people that have supported
my work and career. Ramsay and Candy. Mom and Dad.

Editorial director: Anne Furniss
Creative director: Helen Lewis
Project editor: Lucy Bannell
Art direction and design: Smith & Gilmour
Photography: Martin Poole
Illustration: Blindsalida
Food stylist: Aya Nishimura
Props stylists: Polly Webb-Wilson & Wei Tang
Production: Tom Moore

This edition first published in 2017 by
Quadrille Publishing Limited
Pentagon House
52-54 Southwark Street
London SE1 1UN
www.quadrille.co.uk
www.quadrille.com

Quadrille is an imprint of Hardie Grant
www.hardiegrant.com.au

Text © 2015 Dale Pinnock
Photography © 2015 Martin Poole
Design and layout © 2015 Quadrille Publishing Limited

Cataloguing in Publication Data: a catalogue record for this book
is available from the British Library.

978 178713 045 6

Printed in China